Houser

Pride of America

By Robert Dunn

Copyright © 2006 by Robert Dunn

ISBN 0-7414-3637-X

Published by:

INFINITY
PUBLISHING.COM

1094 New DeHaven Street, Suite 100
West Conshohocken, PA 19428-2713
Info@buybooksontheweb.com
www.buybooksontheweb.com
Toll-free (877) BUY BOOK
Local Phone (610) 941-9999
Fax (610) 941-9959

Printed in the United States of America

Printed on Recycled Paper

Published December 2006

Chapter 1

1901

Mollie Gates had lost few babies and even fewer mothers; she had never lost both. On this warm September night, her patient was weakening at an alarming rate. The baby was larger than Mollie had anticipated, and time was running out. Frowning at the frightened man beside her, the exhausted midwife asked for more wet towels. This was to be the thirteenth child born into the Houser family, and while having many children was not uncommon in the farmlands of Missouri, Sarah Houser was a small woman who in recent years had not enjoyed good health.

Twenty-two years ago, Sarah had lost her first child, Mary Ellen, at birth, and next had the heartbreak of losing baby George before his first birthday. Since then, Mollie had successfully delivered four boys and six girls to the Houser family. Now, the children sat around the fireplace of their farmhouse anxiously awaiting the arrival of their baby brother or sister, unaware of the drama that was playing out in the next room.

Mollie stroked her patient's damp forehead and said, "I know you're tired, dear, but you have to push as hard as you can."

What she lacked in stature, Sarah made up for in fortitude. When Lemuel returned, Mollie was slapping a tiny, wet bottom, and Sarah was breathing short quick breaths.

Seeing his wife so drained of color frightened the weathered old farmer. "Are you goin' to be okay, honey?"

She opened her eyes and smiled up at him. "You go and tell the kids they got a new baby brother."

*   *   *

The Houser's oldest daughter, Effie, proudly held up the infant to the family. "Let me introduce all of you to the world's dearest baby boy, Lemuel Clarence." Effie held the newborn for a few seconds longer, and then handed him to her Sister Martha.

"Can ya believe the size of those hands?" Perry asked.

"How about the size of the baby?" Nancy added. "Should we call him 'Lemuel' or 'Clarence'? If we call him 'Lem', nobody'll know if we're talking about baby brother or father."

William grinned proudly at the new arrival. "'Little Brother' is plenty name enough for me."

"'Little Brother' it is," James echoed."

"This little fella' is the one who has so many names to learn," Perry said.

Nancy suggested, "Why don't we encourage him to call us 'Big Brother' or 'Big Sister' until he gets old enough to use our Christian names?"

The oldest Houser boy straightened up to his full six-foot stature. "I can tell yuh right now, the first time this little guy calls me 'Perry' is goin' to be one dismal day."

Martha placed her little brother in Nancy's waiting arms, and looked proudly at Perry. Twelve to thirteen hour days tending to the farm left the boys little time for formal schooling. A naturally bright woman, Nancy had educated herself through reading the Bible, a McGuffey Reader, and other treasured books in the Houser farmhouse. She had spent long hours teaching her siblings. She would never say anything that might embarrass her older brother, but was proud Perry had chosen the word 'dismal' instead of several slang words that would have been just as appropriate.

Chuckling, she said, "Maybe he'll always call you 'Brother', Brother."

*   *   *

Lem dug down into his overalls' pocket, pulled out three crinkled dollar bills, and handed them to Mollie. "I shure appreciate everything you've done for us."

"Take good care of her, Lem. She should'n be havin no more kids."

"I'll sleep in the barn if there's no other way," he promised.

The midwife giggled. "I think you two'll find some other way."

Chapter 2

January 1904

The sun-chiseled creases in Lem's forehead deepened as the first shafts of morning light spread across the quilt and onto Sarah's face. She was always the first person up in the morning, hurrying around the kitchen creating appetizing aromas of coffee bubbling, bacon spitting grease, and bread frying in a pan. These chores were often performed while dodging her little toddler as he darted around the kitchen. The Houser girls all pitched in and helped, but Sarah ran the household. As Lem pulled on a clean pair of overalls, he could hear his daughters in the kitchen preparing breakfast. No one asked why so many tasks, formerly the dominion of their mother, now fell on her daughters, but furrowed brows and moist eyes revealed concern over the threat of losing the loving-glue that held the Houser family together.

He reached down and patted his wife's cheek. "Why don't you just rest in bed today? The girls are caught up on all the chores around the house."

She tried to push herself up, and then fell weakly back onto the pillow. "I guess I'm not good for nothin' anymore."

He sat back down on the bed. "Don't you go talkin' like that. I can't even imagine what life would be like around here without you."

"You're goin' to get along fine. Our daughters will look after their daddy. We did a good job, Lem. Eleven children still in this world and not a one gone bad."

"Little Brother still needs both you and me. Don't leave us so soon, Sarah."

4

She took his hand. "I guess the good Lord decides those things."

"If you leave, I know you won't be comin' back, but I promise I'll be comin' to you by and by."

"I know you will, sweetheart, and I'll have your favorite apple pie hot out of the oven when you get there."

He placed his knuckles on each side of his nose and wiped the tears sideways across his brown cheeks. "Me and the boys got to get out in the fields. The dirt's not goin' to hoe itself."

*   *   *

The Houser daughters busied themselves milking the cows, churning butter, gathering eggs from the henhouse, grinding coffee, and washing piles of clothes. Neither man nor boy in the family had more than one change of clothing, which called for daily scrubbing to remove the sweat and grime from shirts, socks, and overalls worn the prior day. When the morning chores were completed, some turned to cleaning house, while others peeled potatoes, sliced meat, and picked vegetables from the garden to prepare dinner for the Houser clan. Once dinner was over, and the male family members had returned to the fields, it was time to begin planning for supper.

Evenings, the boys in the family loved to tease the girls, asking, "What were you doin' all day while we been working?"

"Just playin' games and nappin'," was the most common response.

The girls made frequent trips into Mother's bedroom, often just to look at her sleeping and to say a little prayer. If she was awake, the sweet smile she extended almost broke her daughters' heart. Only little brother's constant motion broke the solemnity aura.

Nora raised her head up from the washtub and watched her tiny brother streak past on bare tiptoes close behind the

5

family dog. "How does he do that without fallin'?" she asked Elizabeth.

Catherine brushed her hair out of her eyes, then twisted the handle of the wringer, drying a shirt enough to hang on the clothes line. "It seems no one bothered to tell him about gravity."

Nancy fastened a clothes pin onto another pair of overalls, then stepped into her little brother's path and scooped him up as he tried to go past. "You gots a hug for Sister?"

One quick squeeze and he struggled down to resume his chase. "He never seems to get tired," she observed.

At supper Little Brother asked the question that was on everyone's mind. "Why is Mama still in bed?"

Lem cleared his throat. "Mother is very sick. I'm praying the good Lord doesn't take her from us, at least not for a while."

Little Brother's face looked puzzled. Why would someone who was good take away his mother?

* * *

In spite of the hot July night, Sarah sat in her rocking chair wrapped in a blanket. In her weakened condition, she did more listening than talking. Her pleasant expression contradicted the sadness she felt knowing that she would soon leave her husband and children for the unknown world beyond. After the evening prayers, William snatched up Little Brother, and the boys retired to their bedroom. The girls, one by one, climbed the steps up to the loft. Lem helped his wife out of her chair and into their own small bedroom.

She clung to his arm as he helped her down onto the bed. "I feel so weak. I'm 'fraid I won't last much longer."

"I know. There's been some hard times in my life but nothin that ever hurt like this."

"Dying is part of life, dear. The important thing is I'm ready."

"I'm ready too, but I don't think He's goin' to take me quite yet."

Chapter 3

Grief hung like a black cloud over the family as the Houser brothers carried the homemade wooden casket to the grave dug earlier that day. A grassy area under a young Oak tree about two hundred feet uphill from the farmhouse was the site of the Houser family plot. Mother's gravestone would join two smaller stones that marked the final resting place of her two children who had not survived past infancy. The widowed farmer carried the worn family Bible, and Martha held Little Brother's hand as he and the other family members formed a procession behind the box that carried such a precious cargo.

Before lowering the casket, Lem cleared his throat several times, and then addressed his family. "Y'all know how much your mother loved you. Now she's shut her eyes to this world and opened 'em to one far more beautiful. I want each of you to promise me you'll live your lives as if she was watchin' you, cause I got a good hunch she is. You do that, and she's goin' to look down at you and smile." He took out the old Bible and read the twenty-third Psalm, concluding with, *"I shall dwell in the house of the Lord forever."*

The youngest family member tried hard to understand what had happened. All of the family said his mother was gone, yet they acted like she was in the long wooden box. How could someone be two places at once? Wherever she was, he no longer had his mother with him. He tried without success to hold back the tears.

*   *   *

A lonely hush fell over the family on this first night the Housers gathered for supper without their mother in the house.

"I wish I could take the sorrow out of each one of you," Lem said. "It hurts real bad 'cause we want her to still be with us, but Mother had dreams for each one of you. I don't reckon they included these long, sad faces. You remember how she used to say, 'Every winter is followed by a spring?' She was right, too. She was smarter than lots of people that got more book learnin'."

Martha said, "You know what she would be saying right now? 'What kind of a family did I raise? Haven't I taught you better than to stand out in the rain?'"

"I guess that's what we're doin' all right," Perry added. "We're standin' in a storm of sorrow when we should be pushin' our woe aside and bein' glad that Mama don't have to suffer no more."

"I'll bet she's playing with Jock right now," Effie said. "That old dog always liked her best."

Laughter burst in on the solemn mood at the thought of Mother and their old dog romping around together. The moment of hopelessness was broken. Tears remained to be shed, and sadness would creep up when least expected, but everyone knew the family would struggle through this most difficult time.

"Does dogs go to Heaven?" Little Brother asked.

"I can't see any reason why they shouldn't," Perry assured the toddler.

All eyes rested on the youngest Houser sitting in his high chair. His older siblings pondered the effect of one so young not having a mother. Many smiles, but not one dry eye, could be seen when Nancy took a cotton napkin and wiped off his chin exactly the way Mother used to do.

While the girls were cleaning up the dishes, the boys played their favorite game, each of them sitting on the floor and challenging Little Brother to wrestle them down. Each pretended to put up a good fight before succumbing. The girls suspected it was just family pride that caused bigger brothers to exclaim at the strength of the youngest Houser. Finally, when Perry and Moncy had allowed Little Brother to subdue them, the toddler came tearing at James. William, who had climbed back to his feet, grabbed him before he could get past, tossing him high in the air and catching him on the way down. The smallest Houser bubbled over with giggles.

"Hey, little buddy," William chuckled. "What's your hurry?" He wheeled the youngster around and turned to the girls. "You know who this is? This is my best little buddy."

"Am I your very bestus buddy?" the child asked.

William roared, "Yes you are!" With that he pulled the struggling child to the floor on top of him.

"You two," Martha said shaking her head.

William and his little buddy kept wrestling, not realizing that during this night of grief and frivolity Buddy Houser had inherited a new name.

Chapter 4

April 1910

The pastoral beauty of spring in Missouri always lightened family spirits. Deep blue rivers, where Cherokee Indians once canoed, roared past well-worn bluffs. Green bottomland forests and shimmering gold tallgrass prairies displayed the same splendor as when pioneers in their covered wagons traveled the Oregon and Santa Fe Trails. Whistling and singing, so natural during this season, made workloads seem lighter. Over the years, the empty rocking chair in the main room of the Houser farmhouse had transformed from too painful to behold, to a fountain of sweet sadness and fond memories.

Nancy was now referred to as "Mom" and Martha had acquired the title "Teacher." Eight-year-old Lemuel Clarence couldn't remember being called anything but "Buddy." Other siblings sometimes used their Christian names yet occasionally referred to one another as "Sister" or "Brother." Although most of Lem and Sarah's children were of marriageable age, their commitment to running the farm, and the little chance they had to meet outsiders, kept the family chain unbroken. The farm produced enough sweet corn for the family to sell or trade to keep anyone from going hungry, but provided little beyond the necessities.

Buddy didn't know what it was like to wear clothes that had been purchased solely for him. Four times hand-me-down overalls always started out the day clean, and patches on the knees were of no concern. Shoes were only worn when accompanying his father and brother to work in the fields. Faded shirts, one red and one blue, were ample for weekdays, and why would anyone need more than one white *Sunday-go-to-meetin'* shirt? His waking hours were divided between working and being taught what Nancy called the three "R's", readin', 'ritin', and 'rithmetic. He preferred the former because he could compete with his brothers lifting heavy bags of grain, nailing fence posts, or seeing who could shuck the most ears of corn. Of course, at such a young age, Big Brothers lifted heavier weights and accomplished more, but this only made Little Buddy try harder. "Someday I'm a goin to beat you," he often challenged.

After having Buddy add up several columns of figures and then read *The Little Red Hen* for at least the twenty-fifth time, Martha said, "Nancy and I are going into Clifford to pick up some supplies. Would you like to go with us?"

Buddy's eyes lit up. Going to town was a special treat that didn't come along very often. "Shure Sister, that sounds keen."

Martha frowned. She didn't like her favorite pupil using slang words.

*   *   *

Nancy pulled back on the reins stopping the wagon in front of *Perkins Feed And General Store*. Buddy's feet hit the ground before the wagon quit moving.

Martha looked across the street and saw some young boys. "Why don't you go over there and make the acquaintance of those lads? They look about your age."

Buddy suddenly became very shy. Most of his prior experiences with those his age happened in church and involved kids from other farms, mostly ones he'd known all his life.

"Go ahead, Buddy," Nancy said. "They're not going to hurt you."

The suggestion that boys so small could hurt him aroused his competitive nature, and he marched across the street.

A fat boy about Buddy's height looked him over and said, "I never see'd you in town 'afore."

"I live in Winigan. Name's Buddy Houser."

"Buddy's not a name. It's what yah call someone yah like. I don't like yah that much. Does ever'one in Winigan dress funny as you?"

The youngest Houser looked down at his hand-me downs, and the tape holding his shoes together, and for the first time was embarrassed about how he looked.

Another skinnier boy laughed and said, "See how his eyes'r the same color as his raggity overalls."

With the innate cruelty many boys reserved for strangers, tears forming in the newcomers eyes only egged them on.

The third boy said, "I heered bout the Housers in Winigan. Y'all the ones that ain't got a mother."

Buddy's face flushed, and he doubled up his calloused fists.

The fat boy asked, "What yah gonna do when I rip those overalls offa you?"

Buddy looked at his grinning tormentor, so much smaller than the brothers he'd wrestled all his life, and not any heavier than some of the grain bags he tossed around. The rejection still hurt, but it was now superseded by a challenge. "I don't like to hurt anybody, so it wouldn' be smart for you to try that."

Caution slowed the brashness of the town lad as he saw no fear in the newcomer's eyes. "There's three of us and only one of you."

"I guess I'd jus' have to hurt you one at a time. Hope I don't knock out any of your teeth." It wasn't a threat, just a statement of fact. He was sure that as soon as he sent the fat boy bawlin' the smaller ones would run away.

One of the smaller boy's voice quavered as he said, "Let's us get outa here, Ira. He ain't done nothin' to us."

Ira wanted no part of someone who wasn't afraid of him, especially one with such big hands and wrists. "Were a goin' to let you off easy just this one time."

Tears ran down Buddy's cheeks as he walked back across the street toward the empty wagon.

Walking out of the store, Nancy and Martha were dismayed by their forlorn and tearful little brother.

"What's the matter Buddy?" Nancy asked while pulling her youngest sibling up next to her.

"Why don't I have a mother?" he sobbed. "And why do I have to wear these dumb old clothes that everybody else has worn?"

Nancy and Martha glanced at each other. It was more than clear what had happened across the street.

Martha began to explain some things she knew about and others where she wasn't so sure. "Papa has to choose between us having enough food to eat and buying new clothes. He's got a lot of mouths to feed, and we don't know when this drought will ever end. It's a cold hard fact we don't have much money to spread around. Things aren't always easy to understand. Everybody has to die sometime, but I've asked the Lord many times why He took Mama so soon. The only thing I can tell you is that she and Daddy taught us to be good, decent people, and someday, by and by, we'll all be together again."

When Martha had begun her dissertation, Nancy disappeared back into the store. She soon reappeared with a piece of black licorice candy.

Buddy's tear-filled eyes widened and a grin spread across his face. During the Christmas season, Sister Effie sometimes made chocolate fudge, but store-bought candy was a rare treat. "I don't care what those dumb town boys think, Sisters."

Chapter 5

The Fourth of July picnic was an event the nine-family Congregational Church in Winigan anticipated all year long. Platters of crisp fried chicken, stacks of steaming corn-on-the-cob covered with mounds of butter, several bowls of potato salad, and watermelon cut into quarters lined one long table in the churchyard. As much as Buddy enjoyed the food, the challenge of beating older boys at some of the races and jumps was what made his heart beat faster. Outperforming boys his own age was too easy, but he could still feel the sting of losing the long jump and foot races last year to a long-legged boy named Clayton Wells. This youth, two years his senior, had reminded Buddy several times at church that he was the better runner and jumper. This year the youngest Houser was determined to win all the first prizes.

Although two boys older and bigger than Clayton entered the competition, Buddy won the high jump, short race, and long race with surprising ease, causing his family to erupt in loud celebration. His smile soon turned to a frown as his first two long jumps put him in last place against the bigger boys. He had only one jump left, and the longest mark seemed impossible to reach.

Perry picked up a pitcher and poured himself a glass of lemonade. "I guess he's not happy unless he wins everything," he announced between sips.

"You know who's fault that is," James added. "We've been encouraging him to try to whup us ever since he was in diapers."

Watching all this, Brother William figured out the problem. Buddy didn't have enough weight to carry him through the air far enough to beat the bigger boys. He gathered up several round stones and approached his little brother. "Hey Buddy. Open up your hands." He placed the stones in the center of each hand and folded Bud's fingers over them. "Swing your arms when you're runnin' toward the toe-line, then when you're ready to jump, throw your arms out in front of you. Let's jus see what happens."

Buddy ran enthusiastically to where his other brothers were clapping and cheering. He did exactly as William instructed and, with stone-filled hands out in front of him, sailed past the marks of the other children.

"Wow!" James and Moncy yelled in chorus. "How did that happen?"

William looked toward his grinning little brother, put his finger to his lips, and mouthed, "Our secret."

As Buddy sat at one of the wooden tables and enjoyed his well earned feast, younger boys and giggling little girls crowded around. "All this attention ain't half bad," he thought. "There's nothin' as fun as winnin'," He would ponder the important lesson Brother William had taught him when there weren't so many people around.

When the hot July sun had moved into the western sky, Pastor Henry gathered his flock together for a songfest. The evening was too pleasant to go inside, so guitar and ukulele strumming took the place of Sister Effie's organ music. Patriotic songs, interspersed with hymns, brought tears to the eyes of a few Civil War veteran grandpas. No separation existed between Blue and Grey as all sang songs like, "*America! America! God shed his grace on thee, And crowned thy good with brotherhood from sea to shining sea.*"

Just as the pastor had finished the benediction, a sound like several garbage cans rolling down a hill startled the congregation and all eyes turned in the direction of the road. In a few seconds, a horseless carriage emerged from over the hill and pulled up in front of the church. A portly gentleman with an odd-looking hat yelled, "Anybody know which way to the steamboat landing in La Grange?"

Everyone laughed and several pointed back in the direction from which he had come.

"I told you you were going the wrong way," the lady next to him scolded.

Buddy took off running at first sight of the automobile and was there well before any other children. His eyes widened as he gazed at the beautiful black machine with a shiny emblem that read "*Packard.*" "Will that thing go very fast, Mister?" he asked.

"Over thirty-five miles an hour if I open her up."

By then the rest of the youngsters were staring wide-eyed at this miracle of modern invention.

"What do you think about these new automobiles?" Lem asked his oldest son, Perry.

"I've heard if you get behind one of them, the fumes are pretty foul."

"Worse than horse farts?" Lem asked.

Perry doubled over laughing. "You got a good point there, Pa."

*   *   *

Little Buddy sat on the back of one of the two Houser wagons on the trek back to their farm. The setting sun turned his shadow into the likeness of a giant. He lifted his arm in the air and smiled at how the dark shape could reach clear over to some trees in the distance. What Brother William had shown him today would make it easier to win future contests against the boys at church. His shadow would hardly leave the wagon on the way to the church picnic and look at it now. "Like makin' your shadow longer, beatin' people that are bigger than you just takes some plannin'," he decided.

"You makin' some shadows?" William asked from the front seat.

Buddy smiled at his big brother. "Uh-huh. Look how long I can reach."

"Somethin' tells me yuhr goin to be casting a lot bigger shadows on down the line, Little Buddy."

Elizabeth May began singing *In The Good Old Summertime,* and soon both wagons bombarded the countryside with Houser style music. Though barely in her teens, Liz was already known to have the most musical talent of the family. She played organ, piano, and banjo, and had a lovely singing voice. Singing one song and then stopping was unthinkable, and Perry led out with *Ida, Sweet As Apple Cider.* As darkness closed in, the hoof beats of the horses were accompanied by, *By The Light Of The Silvery Moon.*

After the last song, little Catherine said, "I heard a lot of families in Clifford are puttin' in electric lights."

"I been told they cause freckles," Nora warned.

Chapter 6

October 1910

The Houser children watched their father limping for several days, but whenever one of them asked what was wrong, he said, "Nothin' that can't wait till after harvest."

Tonight, when Effie saw him hobbling through the door grimacing with pain, she sprung into action. "You sit yourself down right now and let me have a look at that leg."

Reluctantly removing his boot and sock, he grumbled, "I can't afford to lose any work time."

The oozing wound her father uncovered made her gasp. "Papa, why did you let this sore fester so long?"

"Because a man's gotta do what he's gotta do."

Martha walked over and looked at his leg. "Oh my goodness, one of you boys better go fetch Doc Baker."

The other children gathered around, each expressing surprise and shock at the red, swollen gash.

"How did you hurt yourself, Pa?" James asked.

"It started out with a blister, and I guess my shoe rubbed it raw."

"It's worse than raw, Papa," Effie said. "I'm afraid it's infected. Catherine, would you fetch me some alcohol and some clean wash rags. I'm going to wash it out as best I can."

*   *   *

The concerned look on Doc Baker's face frightened the younger family members. His countenance was alarmingly similar to what they'd seen just before Mother died. Reaching in his satchel, he handed Effie a brown, glass bottle. "This is Quinine Sulfate. Make sure he gets two tablets every four or five hours, and keep cleaning the wound with alcohol. I'll be back to check on him in a couple days."

Moncy followed the doctor out to his horse. "How bad's Pa's condition?" he asked.

The country doctor sighed. "I wish I could assure you that he's going to be okay, but the poison has entered his bloodstream. Effie did the best thing she could have done but it should have been treated long before now. Sometimes the Quinine works and sometimes it doesn't. We have to wait and see."

"Isn't there anything else you can do, Doc?"

"A few years back, physicians would have cut off his leg once it got this poisoned. Patients usually died anyway, so now we just try our best to treat it."

"What can I do?"

"Just see that Effie cleans the wound regularly."

"And pray?"

The old country doctor sighed. Over many years he had seen the Angel of Death visit churchgoers right along with barroom brawlers and floozies. He believed that God took everyone in their appointed time, but merely said, "It can't hurt."

*   *   *

Moncy wiped the sweat off his forehead and gazed across the cornfield at four gravestones on the hill. Only twelve days had passed since his father had called the family into his bedroom and announced, "Your mother was just here."

Always the practical one, Martha asked, "Do you mean you had a dream about mama?"

Lemuel Lewis Houser smiled wearily. "No dear, Mother told me to say goodbye to the people I love most. It was so wonderful to see her sweet face and hear her voice again. I suspect it won't be long till I'll be steppin' into Paradise, but I'm sorry the good Lord is callin' me right now when we're in the middle of harvest."

William put his hand on his father's forehead. "You're burning up with fever. Catherine, Nora, go get some cold towels."

Lem raised his hand to stop the young ones from leaving. "It's no use. My time's come. Mama and me made sure you all knowed how much we love our children. Well, remember, people die but love don't." Following one small groan, he smiled up at something only he could see. "Darlin', you look more beautiful than you did on the day of our wedding."

Buddy stared down at his father's face. It looked like he was smiling in his sleep, but, the way everyone was hugging each other and crying made him realize Papa was not going to wake up. With that, the youngest Houser burst into tears. He wondered why God didn't like him. All the other boys at church had both a mama and papa. Now he had neither.

Switching his gaze from the family plot to the sweating youngster working next to him, Moncy said, "Slow down, Buddy, I don't need you gettin' sick too."

At a time when help was needed the most, Perry and James had come down with the measles, leaving only he, William, and their littler brother to do the men's work.

Without pausing or looking up, Buddy said, "I ain't gettin' sick."

Looking at the boy working harder than anyone had a right to expect, he said, "Ya know, I believe you."

Moncy continued shucking corn, but his mind was miles away. "I'll be twenty-eight on my next birthday," he thought. "Now that both Ma and Pa are gone, it's time to start huntin' for a wife. Martha and Nancy are great with Buddy, and Catherine and Nora still need some lookin' after, but it isn't fair to saddle them down with all that responsibility. They should be thinkin' about gettin married and havin' kids of their own. Lord knows they get enough looks from the men hereabouts. Most of the girls at church don't interest me that much, but Willis Langdon's youngest daughter... now that's a different matter entirely. From remarks I've been hearing, Grace might have some feelin's for me too." Thinking about the lovely girl who might some day become his bride brought a smile to his face.

Chapter 7

November 1911

Listening to the train whistle's long clear blast, Moncy put his arm around Grace and tried to swallow the lump in his throat. Effie stood alongside her betrothed, Charlie, biting her lip to avoid bursting into tears, while Elizabeth May comforted herself by squeezing the hand of her new beau, Forest King. This was a sad day for the only three members of the Houser family who would remain in Winigan. It seemed unthinkable that a family as close-knit as the Housers would have ever become so splintered.

In the year since father had gone to his eternal home, some difficulties had proved insurmountable. First, the continuing drought had made it hard to keep food in the house. Then, a wealthy gentleman made the kind gesture of offering them a loan. "Just enough to tide you over," he'd said. It appeared at the time that they were in no position to turn it down. Later, they discovered that the loan was due to be paid before the harvest was brought in. The lender never asked for repayment of the note. Their benefactor allowed them to harvest the corn without any knowledge that foreclosure proceedings were already underway. With the loan-shark now owning both the farm and the corn that had been harvested, family members had no choice but to each seek their own separate calling.

The Cash family, who owned a neighboring farm, had taken in the girls. Moncy felt it was partly their Christian generosity but also had a notion it also involved the Cash's oldest son's love for his sister, Effie. This truth of his suspicion came to light soon when Charlie Cash and Effie announced their engagement.

Employment opportunities were scarce in northeastern Missouri causing Martha to accept a teaching position in Oxnard, California. Perry and William also left to seek employment in the Golden State, and within a short time Nancy followed. Jim always had a hankering to be a cowboy and left for Texas to raise cattle. All that held Moncy in Missouri was his love for Grace Langdon and his desire to continue providing a home for his little brother, Buddy. He secured a job selling farm equipment in Clifford and proposed to Grace a few weeks later.

Grace had always been fond of Moncy's little brother and the family of three found happiness in a small house near the Cash farm. Family get-togethers became smaller and many evenings at the Cash farm or Moncy and Grace's little house were spent reliving fond memories.

The letter from Martha had arrived a few days ago telling them she had vowed to be the bride of a wonderful gentleman named Walter Conklin and they were going to open a restaurant near Oxnard. She invited the youngest Housers, Nora, Catherine, and Buddy to come live with them.

"It's beautiful here in California," she wrote. "It's warm all year round and the sun setting in the ocean make one's eyes touch a bit of Heaven."

With such an opportunity waiting, Moncy, Effie, and Elizabeth could only encourage them to go.

Moncy kept one arm around his new wife and put the other around Buddy pulling them both close to him as they watched the last pieces of luggage loaded onto the train.

The conductor called "All aboard," but Buddy didn't move. He loved his sister, Martha, but the only life he knew was here in Missouri. "Can't I stay here with you, Brother?"

Moncy could barely choke out the words, "No the best chances for your future are in California."

"I'm gonna miss you so bad."

"I'm going to miss you too, Little Buddy."

24

Nora and Catherine rushed up to them, "Hurry Buddy, we're going to miss the train."

"Goodbye Effie, goodbye Elizabeth, goodbye Moncy," the younger girls called back as they pulled their little brother toward the waiting train.

Moncy could still feel the warmth of their embraces as the train disappeared in the distance. "Well, I guess it's just you and me in our new house now, honey."

Grace smiled, took the hand she was holding, and pressed it against her stomach. "That's not exactly true, dear."

The sadness was put aside for a moment as Effie and Elizabeth excitedly hugged and congratulated Moncy and Grace.

*　　　*　　　*

The Houser children calmly accepted the conductor's explanation, "Due to a mix-up in reservations, we don't have any sleeping quarters for you." Having a separate place to sleep was a luxury that hadn't even crossed their minds. Seeing mountains, rivers, and lush green fields flash past their windows was so exciting, why would they worry about anything better than this? They happily occupied their assigned passenger seats the entire length of the trip.

Four days later, they climbed down the steps and onto the wooden decks of the Oxnard train station. They quickly sighted the familiar face of Martha, and standing next to her was a tall, handsome man. The grin he wore was almost as wide as the grin on their sister's face.

Chapter 8

May 1921

Sitting on the lawn in front of Oxnard High School, Cliff Argue held up his bag-lunch and said, "I'll trade you sight unseen."

Bud chuckled. "I'm not sure that's such a good idea."

While glancing into his brown paper bag, Cliff asked, "What kinda sandwich you got?"

"Egg salad."

"I've got liverwurst again. Wanna go halves?"

From past trades, Bud knew that Cliff's mom sliced the liverwurst over half an inch thick, put dill pickles on top, and smothered it with mustard. He quickly agreed. After the swap, he said, "See those girls over there? They've been watching us ever since we sat down."

"Get used to it, my young friend. If you don't want the girls chasing you, quit breaking national high school records while you're still wet behind the ears." Cliff was a year ahead of Bud at Oxnard High, and he wasn't going to let him forget it.

"What do girls know about the shot put and discus?" Bud asked.

"More than you think. When the crowds start cheering, it gets everybody's attention, especially if it's someone like you."

"Someone like me?"

"Yeah, maybe you haven't looked in the mirror recently, but you're not the ugliest guy in school. Maybe a close second, but not the ugliest."

Bud chuckled at this friendly insult. "You know how much I hate coming in second."

Cliff glanced back at the girls, bringing on several more smiles. "Any of those young lady's you like?"

"Yeah, I like 'em all."

A wide shouldered kid in a cardinal letterman's sweater with gold stripes on the sleeve walked across the lawn and parked himself next to them. The big letter 'O' sewed onto one side of the sweater had crossed baseball bats with a ball in between. "I see I'm too late for the daily Houser and Argue sandwich swap."

Cliff bragged, "You gotta be on time if you want keep up with us, Ray."

Ray Wilhite, Cliff Argue, and Bud Houser were the best athletes to have shown up in Oxnard as far back as anyone could remember. It was almost unfair to the rest of the high schools in Southern California that they all arrived at the same time."

"You two going to enter the Olympic tryouts in Pasadena this summer?" Ray asked.

Bud almost choked on his last bite of sandwich. "I'm only a junior in high school. They'll have guys from the best college teams in the country."

"To say nothing about the AAU," Cliff added.

"Last I heard, they don't take away any distance 'cause of your age. You've been tossing the shot put and discus as far as anybody in the country."

Bud sighed, lay back on the cool shaded lawn, and looked through the palm branches at the American flag. He was glad his brother, Moncy, had the good judgment to make him come to California.

Ray continued his affable assault. "Cliff here is another matter. He's so slow in the sprints my grandma could probably beat him."

"That's what you think. I beat your grandma just last week."

Bud sat up and grinned at Ray. "Don't you think he'd take a medal in the broad jump?"

"Well, if you get him scared enough he can jump pretty far."

Cliff asked, "Why don't you go out for track next year, Ray? You're small and slow, but who knows? you might take a few fourth place medals."

"Careful my friend, I might come out there and kick both of your butts. Aren't you two afraid of getting kinks in your necks, turning around so far to stare at those girls?"

Cliff said, "They've been ogling Bud the whole lunch hour. I think somebody's been reading his write-ups in the L.A. Times."

"Oxnard girls that read newspapers, what'll they think of next?" Ray said. He looked toward Bud. "I've got a cousin at L.A. High School I want you to meet. She's really a doll."

"I don't know Ray. If she looks anything like you, I think I'll pass."

Ray turned to Cliff. "I hear you're getting a lot of offers from colleges. Have you decided where you want to go?"

"I'm not sure, but Occidental sounds pretty good. If you guys would promise to join me there next year, it would make my decision a lot easier."

"If Bud keeps setting new records, he's going to get offers from all over the country," Ray reminded him. "It's too early for him to make any commitments."

*   *   *

The bus ride to Fillmore gave the Oxnard baseball team time to reflect over their close loss to Ventura last week. It was a bitter end to a two-year winning streak. Now, unless Thatcher High School upset Ventura, the best the cardinal-and-gold could do was salvage a tie for league championship. For most schools that would have been a successful season, but not this team. Since Ray Wilhite and Bud Houser had arrived on campus, the baseball team had finished first every year. No one was happy to share the title, especially when they felt they were the better team. An angry group of players took the field against an outclassed Fillmore squad.

First baseman, Chavez, started out the game with a crisp single to center field. Hofstetter followed with a double all the way to the wall. Rogers beat out a bunt for another base hit, and Bud Houser knocked the first pitch to him over the wall. After Wilhite, Fulton, Bianco, Trexler, and Conway all got on base with still nobody out, Coach Berlin attempted to slow down the avalanche of runs by sending in some reserves. With only twelve players on the squad, that didn't help too much.

Once the Oxnard Varsity finished pounding the hapless Fillmore baseball squad 22 to 6, they learned that Ventura had barely nudged out Thatcher on a controversial call by the umpire.

"Well, I guess we can't win 'em all," Ray remarked.

Bud said, "We can and we will."

"You may be right. We get almost the whole team back next year and Ventura loses some of their best guys."

"I wish they were all coming back. I'd like another shot at them."

The baseball squad filed silently onto the bus for the ride home. One might think they'd lost the game for the lack of any celebration.

"How many hits did you get today?" Bud asked.

Ray counted for few seconds and said. "I had six."

"I had five."

"Yeah five hits in five at bats, and three of em were home runs."

"I wish some of them had been against Ventura last week," Bud lamented.

Trex Treckler turned around in the seat in front and added, "Coach Berlin said we had 23 hits altogether."

Bud noticed the team mascot, young Jimmie Winters, had already fallen asleep. He pointed toward him. "We almost ran the little guy's legs off picking up our bats."

Ray chuckled, "I'll bet the Fillmore players wonder why we were so mad."

"I'm still mad," Bud said with a sheepish grin. "I guess I just enjoy winning 'em all."

"Greedy son-of a-gun aren't you?" Ray said while slapping Bud on the back. "Now when do you want to meet my cousin, Dawn Smith?"

"You never give up, do you?"

"I wonder who he learned that from," Cliff said turning back toward Bud. "What are you going to do this summer?"

"As soon as school lets out, I'm leaving for Corcoran in the San Joaquin Valley. I've got a job loading trucks with bails of hay."

"No vacation time at the beach." Ray remarked. "How much do those bails weigh?"

"About a hundred pounds give or take."

"You do that to get in shape for hurling the shot and discus?"

"I'm doing it for money, but now that you mention it, I guess it is pretty good training. I might take your suggestion and enter the A.A.U. Track meet in Pasadena."

"I'm glad to hear it. Pasadena is very close to Los Angeles," Ray observed.

"So?'

"Haven't you been listening to anything I said? Dawn lives in Los Angeles."

Bud sighed. "I guess I'm going to have to meet your dog-faced cousin just to shut you up."

"I'll take your insults because someday you're going to get on your knees and thank me for this."

Chapter 9

Bud plunged the hooks into both sides of a hay-bale and with a spinning move tossed the bale up onto the bed of a truck. Locals often referred to summer in Corcoran as, "Hot as Hell, but not nearly as much fun." His shirtless upper body had turned brown as a walnut and still developing muscles glistened on his sweat covered back, shoulders, and arms. He watched his Indian co-worker, lift the bale, and with the aide of his knee, push it up to the top row of the stack. The old man was a couple inches shorter than himself, with sloped shoulders, a barrel chest, and biceps that looked like two well-rounded hams. He wondered how a man that powerful would do in the hammer throw. Wiping the sweat off his forehead, he asked, "Were you into any sports when you were in school, Henry?"

"No time for stuff like that. I always had to work."

"Too bad, I'll bet you could have tossed the hammer a mile."

"Guess we'll never know. I hear you're leaving tomorrow."

"Yeah the boss let me off for a few days. I'm going to Pasadena."

"Hope you win your event."

"Fat chance, with all the older guys I'll be competing against."

*   *   *

The bus driver's method of passing slow moving vehicles during the five-hour trip from Corcoran to Ventura kept Bud wide awake. When it appeared he had no room to pass, the bus driver pulled onto the other side of the two-lane highway, pulling back to his own side of the road at the last possible second to avoid a head-on collision. Finally Bud decided to stop looking out the front window. The drive from Oxnard to Pasadena in Walter Conklin's Studebaker would be a lot more enjoyable than this bumpy bus ride.

When Walter's letter had arrived offering to loan Bud his car if he would enter the track meet in Pasadena, it was too good a deal to pass up. He was sure Walter and Martha would like to go too, but leaving the restaurant over a busy summer weekend was not practical, especially now that both Nora and Catherine were married and no longer there to help out. Martha's husband had taken a special interest in Bud from the day he had stepped down from the train and into what was now his world. He took pride in his automobile, to the point where he had converted the stable into a separate house for it. Being allowed to borrow this treasured piece of equipment was a special privilege, and along with it, quite a responsibility.

*   *   *

Both Martha and Walter were at the restaurant when Bud arrived at the house, so he walked downtown to the malt shop next to the Lyric Theater. His question of whether there would be any students at the school's favorite hangout during summer vacation was soon answered when he heard a chorus of feminine voices saying things like, "Hi Bud." "Nice to see you back, Bud."

Quickly glancing at the counter and booths, he noticed none of his buddies were there to offer a diversion. The empty booth he chose was soon filled with smiling Oxnard coeds. The prettiest one was someone he'd never seen before.

"I'm Rose Sickles," she volunteered.

"I'm Bud Houser."

She giggled. "As if you need an introduction."

"I don't remember seeing you around school."

"Did you know you were on the newsreel at the movie next door?"

Bud was used to hearing about articles in newspapers around the country, but this was something new. "Wow. No, I didn't. Is that how you know me?"

Rose just smiled. "When are you leaving for Pasadena?"

"Was that in the newsreel too?"

Again she smiled.

Bud could tell a few other young ladies were waiting for a chance to visit with him, but this one had caught his attention.

Someone put a slow dance record on the Victrola, and Bud impulsively asked Rose if she would like to dance. They walked to the back of the malt shop where the enterprising owner had installed a polished hardwood dance floor.

As they began to twirl around the floor, he asked, "What school did you attend last year?"

Again the teasing smile. "What does it matter? I'll be at Oxnard this coming year. By the way, I'm going to Pasadena tomorrow myself."

"Really?"

"I'm going to visit my aunt for a few days. I hear it's beautiful there, but I'm not looking forward to the bus ride."

*　　　*　　　*

Bud met Rose and her mother at the door, and then carried her suitcase out to the waiting Studebaker convertible.

"Drive carefully, now," Mrs. Sickles called after them.

Rose looked quite striking as the handsome couple drove past crowded beaches and sun-bleached fields on the highway south toward Los Angeles. She didn't seem to mind the wind playing with her hair, and he guessed she was an outdoor girl. He made a habit of avoiding the type of young ladies who went to the beach, but never went in the water.

"Now, do you want to tell me where you came from?"

"I've been here all along."

"That's impossible. I would have noticed you."

"Well, you didn't."

Chapter 10

It was over an hour before the shot put competition, giving Bud time to mingle with athletes he had admired for half of his life. He watched Earl Thompson from Dartmouth tie his own world record in the 120 yard high hurdles.

He was shocked when world record holder for the high jump, Dick Landon of Yale, completed his first jump, then walked over, extended his hand, and said, "Hi Bud, it's nice to finally meet you."

"How do you know who I am?" Bud gulped.

"Don't be silly," Landon said over his shoulder as he walked back toward the sawdust pit.

World record holding sprinter, Charles Paddock, and weight men, Morris Kirksey and Alma Richards, somehow knew him well enough to shout a greeting when he was within earshot. His head was swimming, and he wondered how much nationwide recognition his records in the shot put and discus had actually achieved.

He felt a combination of awe and dismay as a blond-haired mountain of a man walked toward him with hand extended.

"Hi Buddy," Pat McDonald greeted him. "I guess I'm the guy you have to beat today."

Bud's knees felt weak as he looked up at the Olympic Champion and world record holder in the shot put. "It's nice to meet you, Mr. McDonald. I hadn't heard you were going to be here."

"Yep, they sent me all the way from New York to see if you were for real. The papers back home are playing up the David-and-Goliath angle."

Bud shook his head as if trying to wake up out of some crazy dream.

When McDonald walked way, Bud saw a familiar figure halfway across the field. He trotted over and said, "You son-of-a-gun. I haven't seen you since your graduation."

Cliff Argue grinned broadly. "Great to see you. I might have known you wouldn't wait very long to start takin' on the big guys."

"What have I got to lose? Besides, Walter loaned me his car to drive down here."

"Thinka-that; he sent a boy to Pasadena to beat all the grown men. Have you figured out what you want to do when you grow up?"

Bud laughed. "I never thought I'd say this, but I actually miss your insults. Did you sign up with Occidental?"

"Yeah, I'll be there this fall, but today I'm competing for the L.A. Athletic Club."

"So am I. I guess we're on the same team again, my friend."

"Why don't you come to Occidental next year, and we can show the college boys how it's done?" Cliff remarked.

"I just might do that. Looks like I better go over to the shot put ring. Pat McDonald has come all the way from New York to clean my clock."

"Don't let him scare you, Buddy. He puts on his pants one leg at a time."

"And his pants are about three times the size of mine," Bud reminded his friend.

Bud recognized another formidable opponent from photos he'd seen in the newspaper. Reg Caughy, who held the Australian record of 45'2, wasn't as tall as McDonald but was built like a fire hydrant. This was an intimidating bunch of athletes for a high school kid to challenge.

As soon as the competition began, Bud saw nothing but the mark where he had to put the shot to win first place. Lifting all those bales of hay, and then resting a few days had left his muscles crying for action.

Pat McDonald's first toss was over 44 feet. Gus Pope of the National A.A.U. put it out there close to 43 feet. Pope was the reigning world record holder in the discus and just hoped for a second or third place finish in the shot put. A crowd gathered as Bud got ready for his first throw. "Watch his form!" he heard someone behind him whisper. Bud balanced the ball on his right hand, turned in the opposite direction from the chalk line and crouched low toward the ground. As he began turning, he pretended his body was a spring that gained speed as it uncoiled. His body reached maximum speed as he reached the second full turn, his legs gave a mighty push up, and his right arm shot out, releasing the heavy metal ball high into the air. The crowd gasped and then applauded. Bud looked at the spot where his toss landed and wondered what the fuss was about. He hadn't even reached Pope's mark.

Finally, after all contestants had given their maximum effort, it was Bud's final chance to beat these giants that surrounded him. His mind went back to the Winigan church picnic when Big Brother William had put round stones in his hands to compensate for the weight advantage of the bigger kids. He crouched even lower, visualizing his body traveling faster and his right arm and both legs pushing harder than ever before in his life. When he released the ball, he heard a loud involuntary yell come out of his own mouth. His cry was quickly drowned out by the screaming of the crowd. Even Pat McDonald and Gus Pope were smiling and clapping. He could see his mark was beyond their marks, but didn't know how far his toss had gone until he heard the voice on the loudspeaker announce. "Ladies and gentlemen, if you will all look over toward the shot put ring, Bud Houser of Oxnard High School, has just defeated the Olympic Champion and world record holder in the shot put with a mighty toss of forty-six feet and eleven inches."

The grandstands erupted with a deafening cheer.

Bud repeated some long forgotten words. "It sure is fun winnin'."

Other records remained to be broken that day, and soon Bud was just another spectator wandering from event to event. His next goal was the discus record, but that could wait for another day.

Walking across the grass, he spotted the figure of a young lady looking at him. The impact he felt when looking into her eyes almost took his breath away. There were several pretty girls at Oxnard High, but no one like this. She had this confident way she held herself, and the little smile that seemed to say, "Come and get me if you think you're good enough." He looked back to make sure she wasn't casting her spell on someone behind him, which made her laugh and bring one forefinger across the other in the *shame on you* gesture. He knew he had to meet her and hurried forward.

He was almost to her when a middle-aged gentleman in a suit and tweed cap stepped between them and extended his hand.

"Hello, Bud. I'm Dean Cromwell. I coach track at the University of Southern California.

The name was enough. Everyone in the sports world knew about Dean Cromwell. Bud shook the great one's hand, and then looked at the vacant spot where the lovely girl had been standing.

"I know you still have one year left in high school," Coach Cromwell said, "but I want you to know the Trojan family would like to have you come on board. You're going to get a lot of offers in the coming year, but if you plan to settle in Southern California, it's nice to be a hero among your own people."

"Yes sir," Bud stammered. He wondered if the opportunity gained outweighed the one he'd missed.

Chapter 11

Walter had already left for *Martha's by the Sea* to count last night's receipts and prepare the bank deposit. Martha was standing at the kitchen stove cooking pancakes, and Bud was sitting at the table eating them as fast as his sister took them off the griddle. Summer weather started and ended late in Oxnard, so no one was surprised that perfect beach weather would be greeting students on the first day back at school.

The understated affluence of the Conklin house was quite different from Winigan, Missouri, but the slim, dark-haired lady who fixed his breakfast seemed little changed from his pretty childhood teacher. Bud's feet rested on shiny linoleum floors, and the kitchen table where he ate was varnished pine. All other floors in the white frame house, including his bedroom, were polished hardwood, covered with oriental carpets. Large cement porches on the front and side of the house replaced the wooden front porch of his birthplace, while comfortable chairs and porch swings provided more comfortable areas to lounge than the old wooden steps in Missouri. Still Bud had only fond memories of his childhood.

"Sometimes I think you have a hollow leg," Martha said as she stacked three more pancakes in front of her brother.

He held his hand up indicating this last batch would do him.

She sat opposite him, poured herself a cup of coffee, and gazed at the muscular specimen of masculinity her baby brother had become. His thick sun-bleached hair fell down across his forehead and his tanned face made his eyes appear even bluer. Watching him finish his breakfast, she thought, "It's obvious why the prettiest girls at Oxnard High School are all competing for my brother's affection. I wonder how many of them know his addiction to sports leaves so little time for girls. The best part is he seems oblivious to all this attention he receives."

"I need to ask you a question, Sister."

Martha smiled. He had started calling her by her Christian name when he was in his early teens, and then went back to Sister when he saw how hurt she was.

"What was it like the first time you ever saw Walter?"

She thought for a second before answering, then said, "For a few seconds I couldn't catch my breath."

He nodded remembering a similar feeling. "Do you think you fell in love just like that?"

She took a sip of coffee while weighing his question. "No, I knew there were strong feelings between us, but I had to find out a lot more about him before I would let myself fall in love."

"How long did that take?"

She giggled. "To be honest, it probably took about fifteen minutes. Who is she, Buddy?"

"That's the whole problem. I don't know." He told her about the girl in Pasadena and concluded with, "I've tried to figure out a way to find her, but without knowing her name where would I start?"

"Do you think she was experiencing the same feelings?"

"It seemed like she was."

"Then you don't have to find her. She'll come to you."

"But how will she find me?"

Martha put her hand on Bud's. "My sweet, innocent little brother. Honey, don't you realize that everyone who was at the track meet knows who you are?"

*   *   *

This Friday was orientation, which included an assembly in the auditorium and a short session in their homeroom to get class schedules. Regular classes would start on Monday. Bud caught Ray Wilhite going up the front steps of the school, and they walked together toward the auditorium. "You look reasonably fit for a guy that's been lying on the beach all summer," he greeted him.

"You think throwing hay bales around is hard work? I've been out in the blistering heat playing beach volleyball, body surfing, and running about fifty miles."

"Poor baby! You ran fifty miles in only three months?"

Ray grinned. "Give or take. Who do you have for homeroom?"

"Mrs. Gridley," Bud replied.

"Great, now we'll probably be sent to the vice-principal's office every day for clowning around in class." Ray hurried toward the front of the auditorium. "Let's get a seat down front so we can get a better look at the freshman girls that are coming in."

"They're still just kids," Bud reminded him.

"They'll get older."

"You remember when they paraded us in front of the student body the first day of our freshman year?" Bud asked.

"I keep trying to forget."

As the new freshman class stood on the platform waiting to be introduced, Ray jabbed Bud with his elbow. "Look at that cutie fourth from the left in front."

Bud gasped. Rose Sickles was just entering ninth grade. He had slow-danced with an eighth grade girl, and then driven alone with her all way to Los Angeles. She couldn't be over thirteen. "Dear God, don't let her be twelve," he prayed.

"What's the matter?" Ray asked. "You look like you've seen a ghost."

"I think I might have eaten too many pancakes for breakfast."

The principal, Mr. Bannister, introduced the new freshman class, and then addressed the students and faculty.

He began reviewing information almost everyone already knew about construction on the new high school. By March, the estimated completion date, they expected the cash outlay to exceed the staggering sum of $240,000. "We will have twenty classrooms, a new modern library, and the biggest auditorium in town, containing a motion picture projection room." The principal aroused Bud and Ray's interest when he talked about the new athletic field with bleachers for several hundred cardinal-and- gold baseball and track fans, and kept their attention when he talked about a modern new gymnasium for basketball. He lost it again when he began pontificating about the number of student lockers and the long term plans for the fourteen acres of alfalfa fields surrounding the school.

"Blah-blah-blah, are you going to play basketball this year?" Ray whispered.

"Of course, we have a championship to defend. Why do you ask?"

"Well, it's already obvious you're either going sign up to play professional baseball or accept a college track scholarship."

Bud had never considered making a career out of baseball. "You really think I could make it in baseball?"

"What was your batting average last year?"

"It was .565, but I wasn't exactly up against great pitching."

"That's right, but no high school player in California has ever batted for that average, or hit a couple home runs in almost every game."

"How do you know that?"

Ray laughed. "It was in the Oxnard newspaper while you were gone. People are speculating whether you'll end up playing baseball or accepting a track scholarship at some major college."

Bud remained deep in thought through the rest of the assembly. His friend had put an idea in his head that had to be considered.

Walking down the hall toward their homeroom, Ray said, "My Mom's fixing fried chicken tonight. Why don't you come over for dinner?"

Chapter 12

The tantalizing aroma of chicken frying whetted Bud's appetite when he knocked on the door of the Wilhite house.

"Come in Bud," Ray's mother greeted. "My husband can't wait to talk with you."

Having his friends' fathers treat him like someone special was becoming commonplace, yet still seemed strange. Bud noticed one more place setting at the table than he could account for.

"Someone else coming for dinner?" he asked.

"Just family," she said. "Everyone is out on the side porch."

"Grab something cold to drink and come on out," Ray called.

"Would you rather have ice tea or lemonade?" Mrs. Wilhite asked.

"Lemonade will be fine."

The three men had a brief discussion on the possibility of prohibition, now that President Harding had come out in favor of it, and then Mr. Wilhite began asking Bud the usual questions regarding any decisions he had made about his future.

As Bud politely explained that he was still considering his options, a green Packard convertible pulled up in the driveway. Bud's eyes widened and he could feel his heart starting to pound. The girl climbing out of the automobile was the one he'd seen at the track meet in Pasadena.

She walked toward him with that same, *approach me only if you think you're good enough* smile. His assessment the first time he saw her had been confirmed. She was the most exciting girl he had ever seen. She had hair the color of maple syrup, large blue eyes, and skin that would make a baby envious.

"Bud, I'd like to introduce you to my cousin, Dawn Smith."

"I'm happy… ah… pleased to see… to meet you… Ray told me… uh."

Dawn dropped her overnight bag on the porch, took his hand and said, "It's nice to meet you too, Bud."

After a few seconds, Ray announced, "You can let go of her hand now, genius."

Ray's mother broke the spell when she called from the doorway, "Dinner is ready!"

Mrs. Wilhite seated Dawn and Bud on one side of the table across from Ray.

Bud decided, "If this is a setup, it's the best one I've ever had."

When everyone had eaten their fill, Ray's mother suggested, "Why don't you kids go for a walk? It's such a lovely evening."

Before the three youngsters were very far from the house, Ray remembered something he'd forgotten to do, and suddenly Bud was walking down a country road with the girl who'd had the featured role in his recent dreams.

"That's quite a car you're driving," he began.

"My parents gave it to me."

"How did you talk them into that?"

"They had no choice. I had a contract."

He chuckled. "You had a contract with your own parents?"

"When I was starting my freshman year of high school, one of my friends was badly injured in an automobile accident. It frightened my parents, and they asked me to always tell them when I was going to ride in a car with someone. That's when I wrote the contract. It said that I would never ride in a car without their permission, and in exchange, they would agree to buy me a car when I graduated from high school."

"Did your contract specify what kind of car they had to buy?"

"Of course. My dad is pretty clever. If he could find a loophole he would have used it."

"It sounds like you take after him. When did you graduate?"

"I didn't. I'm just starting my senior year."

"So how did you get the car?"

"It's a long story."

He laughed. "You're amazing."

She smiled mischievously. "I'm glad you noticed."

"Are you staying through the weekend?" he asked.

"I'll leave Sunday right after church. School starts at L.A. High School on Monday."

They walked along silently enjoying the balmy air and watching the first chunk of yellow moon peek over the mountains.

"Tonight is almost perfect," he said.

His questions about whether the attraction he felt for her was shared were answered when her hand found his. One little squeeze and a soft sweet smile told him his winning streak might very well continue.

"Are you going to the beach with us tomorrow?" she asked.

"Try and keep me away."

Chapter 13

Somehow it hadn't occurred to Bud that Dawn's soft glowing skin wasn't confined only to her face. He watched her every move as she and Ray's father threw a baseball back and forth. He enjoyed watching her catch everything the senior Wilhite threw close to her, but preferred when she had to run back and scoop the ball from the sand.

Lounging on the towel next to him, Ray said, "Stop drooling and put your eyes back in the sockets. Haven't you ever seen a girl in a bathing suit?"

"Not one like this. I have to admit you were right about Dawn being special."

"Of course I was right. If you hadn't been so pigheaded you could have met her last year."

"Do you think she likes me?'

Ray appeared to plunge deeply in thought. "Probably not with all the guys she has chasing her, but on the other hand, why did she call me and set up this weekend?"

A wide grin spread across Bud's face. "If you're kidding me, I'll kill you."

"If you can take your eyes off her form for a few seconds, have you noticed how well she can catch and throw the ball?"

"I was wondering about that."

"She plays shortstop on L.A. High's girls' baseball team."

Bud looked surprised, "L.A. has a girls' baseball team?"

"It's a big school."

Mr. Wilhite tossed Bud the outfielder's mitt and said, "You take it for a while, she's wearing this old man out."

"See if you can throw one too hard for me to catch," Dawn challenged.

Bud threw one moderately hard, and she caught it easily.

"Come on; pretend you're throwing out a runner trying to steal second."

He gradually worked his way to harder and harder throws, while she kept challenging him. Finally he whistled one at her that was almost full speed.

"Ouch!" she yelled as she dug the ball out of her glove. "Is that any way to treat a lady?"

She ran over and slugged him on the shoulder, "Close your mouth, and don't look so shocked. I was only kidding. You want to go in the water?"

After catching a couple waves, diving under several more, and swimming around in the refreshing green and white surf, Dawn came and stood close to her wet, grinning friend. "Can I climb up on your shoulders?"

"No!" he said. "Absolutely no climbing." He dove under the water, swam behind her, and came up with her atop of his shoulders.

Bud and Dawn participated in the age-old custom of male and female beachgoers' wrestling and frolicking in an innocent yet exciting surf-dance. In spite of her slippery body against his, he knew to be very careful where he placed his hands. Bud finally noticed Mrs. Wilhite holding up a picnic basket, and the couple reluctantly trudged out of the surf.

*   *   *

Ray's mother knew a romance was blooming and insisted that Bud meet them after church for dinner. Things that Bud and Dawn wanted to say to each other were best said while alone, giving Mr. Wilhite ample time to pry stories and information out of Oxnard's most famous athlete.

The sun was still high overhead when Bud carried Dawn's overnight case to her car.

She sat in the driver's seat, and he stood next to her. Neither wanted to say goodbye.

"How far is it to your house?" he asked.

"Sixty miles. It takes about two-and-half hours."

"I want to see you as often as possible."

"Me too."

"Would you think I'm being too forward if I asked to kiss you?"

His face was already close, and she put her hand behind his head and pulled his lips to hers. The thrill of this first kiss propelled his senses into unknown heights.

After catching his breath he said, "Whenever I can, I'll find a way to get to Los Angeles. I'll find someplace to stay whenever I'm there."

"Are you kidding? You'll stay with us; my dad's dying to meet you. I'll be coming to Oxnard too."

"And between weekends, we can write letters."

"I need one more kiss to hold me until the next time I see you," she said.

Peeking out the window, Mrs. Wilhite told her husband, "I think the weekend was quite a success."

Chapter 14

May 1922

Watching green fields and farmhouses flash by the window of the Oxnard bound train, Bud Houser reflected over the amazing thrills the last few years had provided. Converting from an anxious and shy farm boy entering high school four years ago to a young man making headlines in newspapers around the nation seemed too remarkable to have actually happened. However, winning the discus and setting still another world record in the shot put at the National High School track meet at Stagg Field in Chicago had not capped off his high school career as well as he had hoped.

A middle-aged gentleman sitting a few rows ahead of him clutched a newspaper sports-page in one hand and his hat in the other, and walked over to Bud. He grinned and pointed to Bud's picture. "I thought I recognized you when I walked by. Have you seen this newspaper?"

"No sir, I haven't. Is it a California paper?"

"No, you made headlines in the Chicago Tribune."

"I wonder why? I only won two of the four events I entered."

The man smiled at Bud's reserved view of his performance. "I'm from Los Angeles and my friends and I are just hoping you stay in California for your college career. I'm finished with this paper if you'd like to read it."

"Thank you, I would enjoy that." Bud didn't mention that he couldn't spare a nickel to buy his own paper.

He opened the paper and saw the man hadn't exaggerated. There in bold letters across the top of the page was, "BUD HOUSER SENSATION OF INTERSCHOLASTIC TRACK MEET AT CHICAGO." Below the headline he read, "Oxnard Youth Heaves 12-pound Shot 56 Feet in Chicago Contest; His Work Easily The Feature of Big Meet."

He felt embarrassed as he went down the page, "Bud Houser, the mighty youth from the little town of Oxnard, California established a new interscholastic record for the 12 pound shot here this afternoon when he heaved the lead 56 feet in the national championship." He looked around to make sure no one was watching as he finished the column, and then moved his eyes across the page to read another writer's version of what had happened. "GREAT FUTURE FOR HOUSER PREDICTED BY FAMOUS CRITIC" read the headline.

When he was finished reading, he carefully folded the newspaper and placed it next to him. As soon as he had the chance he would sneak it into his suitcase. He sighed, and remembered his disappointment at other times when he had won some events and lost others. He had entered four events at Stagg Field, and took first places in both the shot put and discus but was only able to take third in the hammer throw and fourth in the javelin. In his mind, this performance was unsatisfactory. Four first place finishes would have beaten Washington High in Cedar Rapids instead of tying for second place with Austin Texas.

It was kind of the gentleman who gave him the paper to say that he and his friends hoped he would go to college in California. He had letters from coaches at Stanford, California at Berkley, and the University of Southern California, inviting him to go to their schools. If those were his only options the choice would be much easier, but letters from so many colleges were overwhelming. The schools with the best track programs in the nation, including Harvard, Princeton, Minnesota, and Michigan had all contacted him. California, Stanford, and the University of

Southern California seemed to be the best picks, but he had to narrow it down to one. Each letter made their school sound like the obvious choice. What a huge decision for someone who still felt the sting of embarrassment from when, as a child, he had worn old taped-up shoes.

*   *   *

"Hi, sister," he called as he walked into the kitchen and laid his suitcase on a chair. Martha ran up and hugged him. "You did it again, honey. I'm so proud of you, but you weren't supposed to be home for several more hours."

"I caught an earlier train. Have you got something to eat? I'm starving."

She grabbed him by the hand and pulled him back out the door. "You can eat later. Grab your luggage. We have to get you back on the train."

As they raced down the road in Walter's Studebaker, Martha explained that half the town was coming out to welcome him home. The last train stop before Oxnard was about forty miles south, and it was going to be a close call getting him there before his originally scheduled train arrived.

Bud gripped his hands under the dashboard as his sister rounded a curve at high speed. "Do you think we'll make it?" he shouted.

"You win all your races. I think your sister can win this one."

*   *   *

The roar was deafening as Bud walked down the steps from the train to the wooden platform he'd first set foot on just eleven years ago. A late model Cadillac was waiting near the platform, and two pretty girls from the high school tennis team each grabbed one of his arms and pulled him toward the auto. The Oxnard coeds pushed him into the middle of the back seat, then rested their heads on his shoulders and waved to the crowd. He decided he would leave this part of the homecoming out of his next letter to Dawn Smith. The man in the driver's seat was Mr. Berlin, Bud's coach.

Another member of the reception committee, H.A. Owen, hoisted a megaphone, climbed onto the running board, and began a speech about Bud's athletic fetes. The speech might have been shorter, but listing all of Bud's accomplishments was difficult to condense. At the end, he boldly predicted, "One day the name of our town will be changed from Oxnard to Houser."

This forecast produced shouts of agreement.

Bud wondered how the cheering crowd would react if they knew that inside he was still the youngster holding rocks in his hand trying to out perform the big boys. His big brothers and sisters were the ones who first made him feel special, and he wished they all could share this moment. He prayed that no one would ask him to make a speech.

A makeshift band, combining high school and alumni musicians, began playing "On Wisconsin," the tune to which Oxnard High School's fight song was written. Following a few marches the band switched to the old but still favorite dance melody, "Sweet Adeline." Students and citizens of Oxnard danced to band music in the center of Fifth Street as people walked by the Cadillac shaking hands with their local hero and congratulating him on his most recent wins.

Finally, another member of the welcoming committee, Edward Hofstetter, took the megaphone and announced the order in which the procession would escort Bud to his home. "The official car will be driven by my good friend, Coach Berlin. The two attractive young ladies showering Bud with the affection we all feel have won their varsity letters in tennis. The guards for the car will be other members of the letterman club known to us as the 'O Society'. Next will be the band, followed by seniors, juniors, sophomores, freshmen, and then all remaining 'Friends of Bud.'"

Both the noise level and the dancing continued as the procession made its way down Fifth Street, circled the Plaza, and then headed toward the Conklin's house.

*   *   *

The pride Walter Conklin felt for the accomplishments of the orphan boy he had taken in when he'd married Martha Houser could not have been more intense if Bud were his own son. Bud respected the wisdom of his surrogate father, and was anxious to hear the opinion of someone with more years of experience.

Sitting at the kitchen table munching cold roast beef sandwiches and homemade tomato soup with her husband and younger brother, Martha told Walter about the way Bud had almost ruined his homecoming reception. She detailed how they'd arrived at the Ventura depot, heard the train whistle, jumped out of the car, and ran yelling after the departing locomotive. She recited how forceful she'd been ordering the engineer to wait until she purchased a ticket and Bud boarded the train.

After she finished her story, Bud turned to Walter. "Pops, I'm not sure what I want to do next. Every school that I talk to makes it sound like I would be foolish not to accept their offer.

"How many offers have you received?"

"I would have to count them again, but coach Berlin says I can go anywhere I like."

"I'm sure he's right. Every coach in the country is going to put his best foot forward for you, Buddy, because they know you can win championships for them. Think of how much better it is to have everyone wanting you than just if it was one or two. This way the final choice will be yours."

"If I can ever make a choice." Bud added, and then took a large bite of his beef and onion sandwich.

"It sounds like all of these sales pitches are confusing you. If there was no one telling you about how great their schools are which one would you choose?"

"I would go to USC."

"Wow, that didn't take very long. Does this have anything to do with a pretty little girl that lives just a few miles from the campus?"

Bud laughed. "Dawn's said her father would send her wherever I go."

Then why USC?"

"Their football coach, Gus Henderson, sent me a letter telling me he wants me on the team to eventually replace Leo Calland. He was their captain last year. He said they have a new basketball coach named Turner who has been one of the better coaches up north. I already know that Hunter is a winning baseball coach, and track coach Dean Cromwell thinks he can win national championships the next few years."

"That sounds like some mighty strong reasons to sign up with them."

"It does until you hear what the other schools have to say."

Walter grinned. "Why do I feel there is something you're not telling me?"

"I never could hide anything from you. Dawn's father, Dr. Smith, told me that USC has one of the best dental schools in the country."

"So you want to be a dentist?"

"That's what I have in mind."

"It appears you've already made up your mind. What's holding you back from making your commitment?"

"All of these other schools have been so nice to me it's hard to tell them I've decided against them."

"Buddy, I couldn't be any more proud of you if you were my own son. The fact that you don't want to disappoint anyone shows your character. Along with everything else you've told me, have you considered how nice it would be to finish out your career in the same place you plan to live?"

"Coach Cromwell mentioned it."

"He's right. I know it's hard to imagine your life fifteen or twenty years from now, but, down the line, it will certainly be nice to be well known in your own backyard."

"Thanks, Pops. I'll write a letter to USC tomorrow."

"Why so soon?"

"Coach Cromwell said once I make my commitment, they'll put it in the newspapers, and that will draw in other athletes from around the country. Can you believe that?"

Martha came over and hugged her little brother. Do you know how special you are, Buddy?"

Chapter 15

June 1922

Graduation exercises for the Oxnard High School class of 1922 produced sensations for which few were prepared. Charitable deceptions of nostalgia shared a sobering awareness that those wearing caps and gowns were entering the adult world of responsibility. Saying last goodbyes to friends and sweethearts became more difficult than previously foreseen. Everyone knew this afternoon would be remembered for the rest of their lives. Today the dedication of the new stadium and athletic field would accompany normal graduation day events.

Bud would have preferred to be seated with his friends, family, and classmates in the new bleachers, but the high school principal, Mr. Bannister, had requested that he sit in one of the folding chairs on the platform facing the crowd. He felt out of place alongside the faculty and city officials yet understood the honor that accompanied his discomfort. He sat between two young ladies who were also graduating today, Ruth Weldon, the salutorian, and Esther Delp, the valedictorian. The warm sun and cool breeze made Bud's head nod sleepily as one by one honor students and city officials sermonized on the multitude of opportunities that lay ahead for the class of 1922.

Suspecting he might be called upon to speak, Bud became fully alert as the subject shifted from commencement to dedication of the new athletic facilities.

Principal Bannister droned on for several minutes about the history of Oxnard High School, and then began enumerating Bud Houser's incredible record of victories and high school, national, and international world records.

Bud was mentally going over the words he would say when a truck carrying a sign pulled through the gate, drove onto the grass near the track, and stopped in front of the platform. The sign for the new field was covered with a tarpaulin.

With a big smile, Mr. Bannister gestured to the truck driver to remove the cover. Bud gasped and the crowd roared as the words on the sign came into view,

"BUD HOUSER FIELD."

An honor such as this was normally bestowed years after the honoree had departed, if not posthumously. Naming the new athletic field after a student before he had even been given his diploma was breaking new ground.

Tears ran down Bud's cheeks as his mind traveled back twelve years ago to the day his father had died, and he had asked why God didn't like him. Perhaps God liked him a little bit after all.

Somehow he gained enough composure to mumble a few words of thanks. Those assembled didn't expect eloquence; Bud Houser's accomplishments spoke far louder than anything he could say.

*   *   *

The malt shop next to the movie theater was packed with seniors, some celebrating their graduation from high school, while others carried on subdued conversations. "We'll stay in touch," and "I'll write to you," were among questionable vows old friends and high school sweethearts shared.

Ray and Bud each dropped a nickel on the counter as the young waitress placed two colas in front of them.

"Ain't it hell being broke?" Ray complained as he showed Bud his last dime.

"Having money must be better, but our time will come."

"So you decided on the University of Southern California?"

"Final choice," Bud confirmed. "I might as well stay with cardinal and gold now that I'm used to those colors. Have you decided where you're going?"

"I've received a few letters from minor league baseball teams, and Occidental College would like to have me pitch for their team next year."

"Cliff Argue would be glad to see you if you decide on Occidental."

"We had some good times together at dear old O.U.H.S." Ray admitted.

"Yeah we did. I imagine the other schools in the league won't shed any tears about our leaving."

Ray chuckled. "I'll miss kicking their butts every year."

"I'm sure you will be striking out other teams' batters for a few more years."

"It will be harder without you getting six or eight runs every game."

"That sounded almost like a compliment," Bud remarked.

"I've been slinging insults your way ever since you arrived here from Missouri, so I guess it's time to set the record straight. I meant every one of them." Ray's moist eyes gave away the affection he felt for his best buddy.

"I would not have expected any less, my friend."

"Have you told Dawn about your decision."

"I just put a letter in the mail, so she won't know for a day or two. They have an outstanding art school. I'm pretty sure she's wanted to become a Trojan all along."

"Well, that makes your decision all the wiser."

Bud looked around the malt shop at all the smiling faces and sad eyes. "You realize nothing will ever be the same after today."

Ray lifted his cola glass. "Here's to new beginnings."

Chapter 16

The Los Angeles station was crowded when Bud climbed down off the train. Even the hour or two he would spend in the cool Los Angeles air would be refreshing after laboring through another hot summer in Corcoran. Summer was never the best time of year in the San Joaquin Valley, but at least it had put some money in his pocket for his first year at the University of Southern California. Dawn had already enrolled in art school and had classes today. This short delay would make their reunion all the more exciting. As he walked toward the ticket window to check when the Pacific Limited was scheduled to leave, he was approached by three young men also carrying luggage.

The largest of the welcoming committee stuck out his hand and said, "I'm Norman Anderson. All my friends call me Swede. These two sorry-looking characters with me are Otto Anderson, no relation to me thank the Lord, and Yale Martz. We'll be going with you to New York, and then we'll be helping you and the other Trojans win the national championship in track this year."

Accustomed to people recognizing him, Bud was not surprised that part of the group with whom he would be spending the next several days knew who he was. "Nice to meet you fellows. What events do you compete in?"

Otto put his hand on the big guy's shoulder. "This monster is the one you'll be regularly whipping in the weight events. Yale here runs the sprints, and I run the hurdles."

60

"You guys certainly seem in a happy mood," Bud remarked.

"Have you looked at our schedule?" Yale asked. "We're going to be seeing the Great Salt Lake, boating down the Mississippi River, spending a day in Chicago, attending a boxing match in New York, and the L.A. Athletic Club is footing the bill for everything."

"I must have been given a different schedule," Bud said. "I didn't see all those things."

"Yale didn't tell you the best part," Swede added. "We have three days to kill in New York before the track meet."

Bud nodded and grinned, "Sounds like we're going to have a great time."

*   *   *

During a train stop in Chicago, the young Trojans went on a sightseeing tour of the city, strolled through Lincoln Park, and then took time for a workout at Stagg Field. Bud was putting the 16 pound shot out over forty-seven feet, and flinging the discus about one hundred forty-five feet. According to what he'd been reading in the sports pages, both distances should give him an excellent chance to win first-place medals against the older and larger men he would be competing against. His new friends, while not achieving times or distances that would guarantee any first-place finishes, seemed in fine shape to give the easterners plenty of competition and, at the very least, take home some second and third- place medals. Not bad, since they were competing against the best athletes in the country, many whose college careers were far behind them. Optimism ran high as they reboarded the Pacific Limited for the last leg of their journey.

Otto stared out the window at a boat steaming down one of the many rivers they had crossed and said. "I wonder when I'll get another chance to see the United States like this."

"With me, I don't think it will be anytime soon," Yale responded. He turned to Bud. "I heard you've already been back East once."

"I've never been to New York, but the City of Oxnard scraped up enough to send me to the High School A.A.U. meet in Chicago last year. People up there don't have much money to spare, so it was quite an honor."

"I'm sure you'll be taking several more trips," Swede added.

"I hope we all do," Bud replied. "How are we going to make the most out of those extra days in New York?"

Otto, Yale, and Swede glanced at each other, and then all seemed to get very interested in the scenery flashing by.

"Is there something you guys want to run by me?" Bud asked.

Otto said, "Well, Swede here had a pretty good idea."

"Wait a minute," Swede said. "I think Yale brought it up first."

"Hey, all I said was I hear Canada is beautiful this time of year."

"I guess we all kind of agreed that an excursion up north would be fun," Otto said.

"A trip to Canada? Are you guys sure we have time?"

"Here's the deal," Otto said. "There is a train that goes up to Canada to some great hiking spots, and on the way back it stops at Niagara Falls. If we're real careful how we spend our food allowance, and stay in an inexpensive hotel in New York, I think we can swing it."

"You guys are sure we have time?" Bud repeated.

*   *   *

A cheer went up as Bud unwound out of his crouching position, spun quickly around, launched the shot put into the air, and then hopped on one foot to keep his balance and not go over the chalk line. They all became quiet when the official marked the spot at under forty-two feet. Most people in the grandstand knew how far this handsome youngster had pushed the shot put in past track meets and were waiting for him to set still another record. What they didn't know was how tired he was or how numb his body felt. Many weight-men in the country would be happy with that distance, but for him this was a disappointing effort, and probably not good enough to win any kind of medal against the competition he would be facing today. He had to do better in at least one of his two next throws. Swede Anderson's first toss was only 136 feet 5 inches, but he knew his best chance at a medal was in the hammer throw.

He and his friends had drug their tired bodies into their hotel room at 3 AM this morning. The trip up north had been even more exciting than they had expected. The scenery on the hiking trails in Canada was breathtaking, and Niagara Falls was the highlight of their journey. Eating at the least expensive restaurants they could find allowed them to each invest fifty cents for a three-hour cruise on the *Maid of the Mist,* where Swede Anderson met the girl of his dreams. His long goodbye to the wonderful young lady he might never see again caused them to miss their train and eventually end up on the night train back to New York.

After Bud's third attempt at the shot put fell short, the first place winner, Pat McDonald, walked over to him.

Putting a huge hand on Bud's shoulder, he looked down at him, "Good to see you again, kid. After you whipped this old man in the track meet in Pasadena, I'm surprised you didn't have better marks today."

Bud was embarrassed to tell McDonald the reason for his lethargy and said, "Forty-five and a half feet would win most meets. You pushed it out there a half-inch short of forty-seven feet."

"I feel pretty good about today but the Olympic tryout is the one that counts."

They stopped and listened to voice on the loudspeaker. "We have the final results in the sixteen-pound shot put. Pat McDonald of the New York Athletic Club is first with a toss of forty-six feet eleven-and-one-half inches. Second is Hills of Princeton, and finishing third is Wander, also of the New York Athletic Club. Bud Houser of the Los Angeles Athletic Club finished fourth. An interesting note – the difference between first and fourth places was only one foot six inches."

The disappointment Bud felt in not winning the shot put carried over into the discus ring. His grogginess while competing in the shot put had been replaced with aching muscles from the steep hiking trails in Canada. After his first two tosses, it appeared he wasn't going to take home a medal in that event either. Preparing for his final toss, he looked upward and pleaded, "Lord, help me to do the best I can with what you've given me." His toss soared well beyond most of the small markers on the grass, and it looked to the crowd like he had pulled out the winning throw on his last effort. The cheering died down when it was announced, "Bud Houser, the teenage great from California, has tossed the dish one hundred forty-one feet five inches to finish a close second to Gus Pope of Portland Oregon.

Swede Anderson finished far behind and seemed even more tired than Bud as the disappointed athletes walked over to watch their buddies compete in the sprints and hurtles.

Yale Martz started the hundred yard dash like he'd been shot out of a cannon, and Bud and Swede yelled at the top of their lungs cheering him on. At the fifty yard mark, it looked like he might save-face for the Los Angeles Athletic Club, but toward the end of the race anyone watching could tell he'd run out of gas, uncharacteristic for someone who was known to be a strong finisher. He finished well back of the medal winners.

Later, in the 120 yard high hurtles, Otto Anderson knocked down two hurtles and also failed to win a medal, however, another team member from Los Angeles, Earl Thompson, won first place in that event.

Sitting on the grass watching people file out of the grandstands, four downcast athletes testified as to how none were at their best on this day that the reputation of California athletes had been trampled on. To rub salt in their wounds, the announcer repeated, "Ladies and gentlemen, once again, the team winners are New York Athletic Club first, Illinois Athletic Club second, and Chicago Athletic Club third."

"How did our other guys do?" Swede asked.

"Flint Hammer won the Javelin, and you guys watched Thompson win the hurtles." Otto said.

Yale added, "If Bud had won the shot and discus, and the rest of us had just won seconds or thirds, that would have given us four firsts and seven medals total. We might have won the meet."

"That's right, and if ifs and buts were candy and nuts, we could throw a great celebration tonight," Swede said. "I can't wait for football season. I'm ready to bump heads with some people."

"Go easy. One of them will probably be me," Bud said. "I'll be on the freshman team this year. By the way, I don't think we should mention the Canadian trip to anyone."

They all nodded agreement.

Yale stood up and stretched his sore muscles. "Well, I guess we better shower and get ready for the awards banquet tonight," he said.

"That should be a lot of fun," Otto growled.

Swede painfully pushed himself to a standing position. "You guys probably won't believe this, but I don't know if I'll be able to eat anything."

"I saw on our schedule they're serving lobster salad and T-bone steak," Bud remarked.

Swede's eyebrows shot up. "Maybe I'll be able to choke something down."

Chapter 17

October 1922

Bud looked from the freshman huddle into the intense eyes of seven big men on the varsity line and two smaller but faster players' right behind them. It was bad enough scrimmaging against athletes a couple years older, but the Trojans still had some battle-tested World War I veterans on the roster. Adams, the big center, was flanked by Callard and Newman at guards; His friend, Swede Anderson, along with Johnny Boyle were the varsity tackles, and Davis and Pythian were crouched at the end positions. Lying on the grass between them lay the big, awkward pigskin. Measuring twenty-eight and a half inches around the ends and twenty-three inches around the middle, the slick piece of leather was not the easiest kind of ball to throw, but what other option did he have? One thing was certain; the frosh running backs weren't going to run through these guys. The fullbacks, Galloway and Tiernan, would be charging in right behind the linemen. A bunch of kids who were in high school last year were trying to block nine of the eleven players on what was considered by many to be the best defensive football team in the country. He leaned toward the circle of first-year players and called, "Eight fly on two; see if you lineman can slow down these apes until I can get the ball away."

He stood about four yards back of the freshman center, with his hands outstretched, and barked out, "Set, at one, at two."

If any time elapsed between the ball reaching his hands and Trojan linemen hitting him, he wasn't aware of it. He waited until the men on top of him unpiled, then climbed gingerly to his feet, noticing that the varsity halfbacks, Roy "Bullet" Baker and Otto Anderson, were playing less than five yards back from the line of scrimmage.

Back in the huddle he said, "Okay, I know these guys are big and tough. They beat USS Mississippi twenty to nothing just last week. If you can't block them, at least get in their way for a couple seconds. Let's try to go the other way; nine crisscross on three…make that on four. We'll see how patient they are." He whispered to his center, "Put the ball a couple feet to my left."

It looked to the defense like a bad snap from center, but Bud took a quick step, pulled the ball against his body, and raced toward the sideline. Left end, Richard Emmons, sprinted down the field and cut to his right. On the other side, right end, Ben Gerpheide, was cutting as fast as he could to the left. Bud twisted out of the grasp of one tackler, eluded another, and with a flick of his wrist floated the football into the hands of a wide open Gerpheide. The grinning freshman sprinted down the field into the end zone well ahead of Baker and Anderson. In five minutes, the freshmen team had done to the Trojan Varsity what the sailors from the Mississippi had failed to do in 60 minutes.

Freshman coach, Hess, looked at varsity coach, Gus Henderson, and said, "If I hadn't seen that, I wouldn't believe it."

Henderson grinned, which was not what players or spectators expected from the man they called "Gloomy Gus." "He threw the ball forty yards down the field without even breaking stride and he was running to his left."

"And it was a perfect strike. I wonder how far he could throw it from the right side of the field if he had time to set up," Hess added.

The referee looked toward the sideline to see if the coaches wanted the Frosh to try the extra point and when he received the go-ahead, set the ball down on the five yard line.

The snap from center was a little high, but Bud pulled it down and drop-kicked it just over the outstretched hands of charging linemen and between the goal posts.

*   *   *

Trudging from Bovard Field toward the Sigma Chi House, Gerpheide was in a celebratory mood. Bud's mood was not as cheerful.

"Bud, we're pledging what I think is the best frat on campus; we just scored on the varsity football team, and you're cozy with a gorgeous coed. Why is it I don't see you smiling?"

"Unless I make some changes, I could flunk out of dental school."

"The course is that hard?"

"It's plenty hard, but my problem is I never have time to study."

"You really have your heart set on being a dentist?"

"Dawn's dad, Dr. Smith, told me that he knows a recent USC grad that made three thousand dollars in his dental practice the first year, and he's heading toward five thousand this year."

"That's a pretty good reason to continue on. What changes are you thinking about making?"

"I'm not sure. When I agreed to come here, I had two goals. One was to get my dental degree, and the other was to go to the 1924 Olympics."

"I didn't hear you say anything about football."

"We only had intramural football at Oxnard, but I've always loved playing the game. Let's face it. We're not really playing any kind of real schedule. While we're on the freshman team, scrimmaging the varsity is the most action we'll get. Maybe it would be better if I wait until I'm a sophomore to play football."

Ben was silent for several seconds as they rounded the corner and turned down 28th Street. "That would free up about twenty hours a week for you to study, but it would be a lot less fun without you there. When are you going to tell the coaches?"

Bud laughed. "I just now decided what to do. Seriously, though, I think they'll understand my problem."

Bud and Ben walked through the dark, empty dining hall and into the kitchen where Sigma Chi's long-time cook, Claire Kennedy, had left out more food than even two ravenous athletes could eat. They both heaped their plates with roast beef, mashed potatoes and gravy, and string beans.

Chapter 18

Bud stepped up onto the running board, climbed into the green Packard Twin Six, and kissed the driver. A whistle from the Sigma Chi house caused Dawn Smith to thumb her nose at two of Bud's fraternity brothers waving at the couple from an upstairs window.

"Hey, be careful. I'm still a pledge you know."

She tossed a small envelope onto his lap before speeding too fast down 28th Street, and then only slowing down at the stop sign on Figueroa. "Speaking of pledges, read this."

Holding onto the dashboard with one hand while holding the envelope with the other, he pretended that any important information must be contained on its face. "Miss Dawn Smith, 4104 West Pico, Los Angeles California, this is very interesting."

"Read the inside, you nut."

"Oh, is there something inside?" He made it look difficult removing the card, then read, "Delta Gamma invites you to tea at the Fraternity Lodge, 920 West 28th Street, Friday from 3 to 5 o'clock. Is Delta Gamma a women's fraternity?"

"As if you didn't know. Because most fraternity boys can't remember two Greek letters strung together, you've probably only heard it referred to as Dee Gee."

"Pull the car over to the curb," he requested.

When she had parked on Figueroa Street, he took her in his arms. "Now that we're away from those voyeurs at my frat house, let me greet you properly."

Some cars honked as they drove by, but the affectionate couple ignored the traffic.

He was holding her just as close as always, but she detected something different.

"The Dee Gees are lucky to get you. Does this mean you'll be living right down the street from me?"

"Of course. Dad will surely go for that."

"You could explain how inconvenient it is to drive your Packard two-and-a-half miles from Pico Boulevard to the campus every day."

"That should work."

Why wasn't he smiling at her the in same way? Dawn reached her foot toward the starter, but Bud stopped her.

"There is something I need to talk to you about before we go."

"That sounds pretty serious."

"I met this guy in my Religious Lit Bible-class. His name is Carl Didrickson."

"Uh oh!" Her face turned crimson.

"He told me about this exciting art student he took to a Phi Mu Fraternity dance at Hollywood Country Club a couple weeks before I got here. He brought her flowers and pretty well filled up her dance card, and said he had a terrific time. Funny thing, she drove a green Packard Twin Six. You remember a couple months ago when I was at your house riding a bike with you on the handle bars, and you kept falling back into my arms and saying how much you cared about me? I guess I assumed I was the only guy in your life."

Tears appeared on her cheeks. "Oh Bud, this isn't like it sounds. Carl is just a friend."

"So, he didn't kiss you good night?"

"He tried, but I told him I was in love with someone else."

He held both of her hands, and they looked intently into each others' eyes.

Finally, he reached out and stroked her hair. "Funny, he gave me that same story."

"I know I shouldn't have gone. It's dreadful having you angry at me."

"I'm not angry, but I'll confess, it was an eye-opener." He reached down, removed his Sigma Chi pledge pin from his sweater and balanced it on his open hand. "If you accept this, it means we're pinned and you can't date anyone else, even if I'm gone to Paris for the Olympics."

She wiped the tears off her cheeks. "If you go to Paris, I'm going with you."

He tried to hand her the fraternity pin, but she stopped him.

"I would rather you put it on me this first time."

He stared at the soft swells in her cashmere sweater and tried to hold his hand steady as he fumbled with his task.

"That little pin shouldn't be too hard to handle for a guy that throws the sixteen pound shot, and you really don't have to be that careful; I don't have anything on my body that will break."

"You are a little imp," he declared. "I see I'm going to have to keep my eye on you."

"How about me keeping an eye on you? Every girl in the freshman class would like to date the handsome and famous Bud Houser."

Driving toward downtown Los Angeles, the bumper-to-bumper motorcars maneuvering their way around bright red streetcars was a stark contrast to the green fields and sandy beaches around Oxnard. Fortunately, Dawn was used to battling the traffic. The L.A. train station appeared to be the hub of urban activity. Just driving past it made Bud glad for the relative seclusion of the USC campus. He heard the whistle of a train and then the powerful "huff-huff" of a locomotive. Dawn continued down Main Street to 9th and pointed out her dad's dental office right over Hardaway's drug store.

*   *   *

It didn't take long at the Lincoln Park roller rink to discover that Dawn was the better skater. Actually, Bud had only skated on sidewalks around Oxnard before he reached his teens. Skating on a slick hardwood floor after all these years would take some practice.

"You played on L.A. High's championship baseball team and you skate quite well. How many other things will I learn about your athletic skills?" he asked.

"I was on the Sunday School Athletic Federation's championship basketball team last year."

"Wow, I don't know if I should be pinned to someone who is better than me at sports."

She pushed him, causing a comic flailing of his arms before pretending to lose his balance and sitting on the polished hardwood floor. When he took her extended hand, instead of helping him up she pulled herself down, pushed him onto his back, and grinned. He caught the sweet aroma of Blackjack gum she was chewing.

"I promise to go easy on you in any contests we might engage in," she promised.

"That's very generous of you. Now, if you'll let me up, I might buy you an ice cream cone."

As he started to sit up, she placed her hand against his chest and pushed him back to the floor. "Might buy me ice cream isn't good enough. You're negotiating with the girl who got a new car just for being good."

"Okay, I promise to buy you ice cream if you will let me up."

"Double decker chocolate and strawberry?" she asked.

"Whatever it takes."

"Okay, that sounds like good deal. I'll release you."

Once on his feet, he wrapped his arms around her and skated over to the rail without letting her feet touch the floor.

"You big fake," she squealed.

"Not really. I'm normally quite clumsy on roller skates. You're lucky to have avoided serious injury."

Chapter 19

Few experiences in life are more exciting than the first year of college, especially if you're in love. Hours freed up from dropping off the freshman football squad allowed Bud to catch up in his dental classes as well as enjoy his new found freedom. On Saturdays, Dawn parked her car in front of the frat house and they walked to Bovard Field to watch Trojan varsity's home football games. Afterwards, they grabbed a bite to eat at a small restaurant on Figueroa, and then hopped from men's and women's fraternities attending dance parties. More than once, they danced one or two dances and left, preferring their quiet conversations on the porch of the Sigma Chi House to the roar of the post-game-crowd. Sundays often started at the Pico Avenue Christian Church and ended up on the beach.

One day, Bud and Dawn took the Pacific Electric train to Mount Lowe for an outing in the mountains. On another cool evening they caught the auto races at L.A. Speedway. They watched "Paleface" with Buster Keaton at a theater near the campus and attended concerts at the Hollywood Bowl. It didn't take long to discover the, "Once a Trojan, always a Trojan" spirit so infectious on campus.

By Thanksgiving Bud was already grabbing off spare time to practice the discus and shot put. It was on the practice field that he met track star, Leighton Dye, to add to the list of good friends he would be competing with for the next few years.

A letter he'd recently received at the Sigma Chi House had once again brought uncertainty into his life. His .550 plus batting average while at Oxnard High School had not gone unnoticed. The Chicago Cubs had offered him a contract for more than he could make in his first two years of practicing dentistry with the promise of even more to come. His decision about which school to attend was still fresh in his mind, and his resolve to participate in the 1924 Olympics, graduate from dental school and begin his practice was still intact, yet how could someone ignore an opportunity like this?

The pledges and members of Sigma Chi were about evenly divided about what he should do. He hadn't even mentioned it to Dawn.

The early morning sun was at his back as he flung the discus out farther than anyone else in Southern California could match. Being the best in this part of the country was satisfying, but who knew how far some of those big guys up north could toss the dish? Working out at this early hour on a Thanksgiving morning was not his preference but he had a big day ahead of him. Dawn planned to take him to Pasadena's Rose Tournament Stadium to see the Trojan football squad play the Washington State Cougars, then on to her parents' house for Thanksgiving dinner.

As he squatted low to the ground preparing for the next spinning toss, he caught sight of someone heading toward him. The large dusky man looked familiar but he couldn't place where he had seen him. When recognition took hold he could hardly believe his eyes. He had never seen Jim Thorpe in person, but everyone knew the big Indian whom most still considered to be the greatest athlete of all time.

"Hi Bud; you have time for a little chat?"

"Of course I have time. I can workout anytime but how often does a guy get a chance to talk to someone like you?"

Thorpe smiled. "I'm in town for a few days and wanted to talk to the young man who might take my place. I've been following your career and we have a lot in common."

The two men walked slowly toward the grandstand and sat on the front row.

"I guess you began getting a lot of attention before you went to college," Bud began.

"You know what it was like; a poor boy from the country with work calluses on my hands before I was ten. I grew up in the Sac and Fox Tribe and somehow figured out I had to get an education if I ever wanted to amount to anything. While I was at Carlisle Indian School in Pennsylvania people began noticing me." Thorpe laughed. "Believe it or not, the first time I was invited to participate in a sport was when I picked up a football the team had let roll over near where I was walking. I didn't even try to kick it that hard but it sailed over everybody's head. I guess you had the same feeling when you found out you could put the shot and fling the discus farther than anybody else."

"I'm not there yet Mr. Thorpe."

"Just call me Jim so I won't feel so old."

"Okay Jim, it must be wonderful being the only man in history to win the Olympic Decathlon and then play both professional baseball and football?"

"On the contrary, I feel quite foolish."

Bud frowned. "I don't understand; you've done it all. What more could you have accomplished?"

Thorpe put his hand on Bud's shoulder. "I guess everybody knows the Olympic Committee stripped me of my medals because, once when I was a little short of money, I had played semi-professional baseball for few dollars."

"That doesn't matter; everyone knows what you did at the Olympics and what you've done since."

"As a pro, I couldn't play college sports either. That's when I dropped out of school." Thorpe stopped talking and looked at Bud.

"Did you hear I received an offer to play baseball for the Chicago Cubs?" Bud asked.

"No, but I'm not surprised. What are you going to do?"

"I haven't decided yet."

"What are you studying?'

"I'm going to dental school."

"Tell the Cubs you're not interested."

"Why?"

"I don't usually talk this much, but I don't want you to repeat my mistake. I've got maybe four or five years left in the NFL, if I'm lucky, and then what am I going to do? I'm not making that much money and by the time I'm washed-up my knees will be too bad to go back to farm work. I'd give up everything right now to have a dental degree. You have the talent to do everything I've done, but where will that leave you ten years from now?"

*   *   *

Dr. Smith bragged about how no one could roast a turkey like his wife, while helping himself to another slice of juicy white meat and smothering it with homemade cranberry sauce. "How did you kids enjoy watching gloomy Gus's Trojans kick the stuffing out of Washington State?" he asked.

"I think we're lucky they didn't figure out our weakness," Bud said.

"Really?" Dr. Smith asked. "Forty-one to three sounds like our boys don't have many weaknesses."

"Yes, but did you notice how, when we were on defense, we always had all eleven men within ten yards of the line of scrimmage?"

"So what would you have done if you were the Cougars coach?"

"Throw more passes. Five quick steps by one of their ends and nobody could have caught him."

Not willing to concede anything, Dawn's father mentioned, "It's not like throwing a baseball. That pigskin is big and awkward. I don't know if it's harder to throw or to catch."

"Before I quit the freshman team, Ben Gerpheide, our freshman right end, would run pass patterns and I could complete four out of five of my passes to him from twenty-five to forty-five yards down the field."

"I'm sure you could, but Washington State doesn't have anyone with your arm on their team."

"Neither does our team," Dawn said.

Are you planning on playing next year?" Dr. Smith asked.

"I don't think so."

"You never mentioned that before," Dawn announced.

"I just decided today."

"Any special reason?" she inquired.

"I want to win the Olympics and I want to graduate from Dental school. I believe trying to play all the sports might ruin my chances, at least my chance to become a dentist."

Dr. Smith said nothing but could not contain his happy smile as he helped himself to another helping of turkey-dressing smothered with gravy.

Bud had already stuffed himself and was wondering how long it would take before he had room for the pumpkin pie he'd seen in the Smith kitchen. "I talked to Jim Thorpe today," he casually mentioned.

For a moment there was complete silence around the dining table, and then Dawn's younger brother exclaimed, "Wow, how did that happen?"

"He came to see me while I was working out this morning."

"That's quite a compliment that he would go out of his way to meet you. It's interesting how you decided to only pursue one sport right after meeting the world's greatest all around athlete," Dr. Smith said.

Bud noticed his future father-in-law looked more pleased than surprised. "He's not only a great athlete; he's a very wise man. He's the one who convinced me to figure out what is most important in my life and then pursue it with all of my energy."

"And what is most important?" Dawn asked.

"Why it's you of course," Bud answered.

She smiled, "You got that one right."

Dr. Smith leaned back and patted his protruding stomach. "Is anyone else ready to take a long walk?"

"I'll have dessert ready when you get back," Cora Smith said.

Chapter 20

Since 1902, when the University of Michigan football team concluded Pasadena's Tournament of Roses festivities by stomping all over Leland Stanford University 49 to 0, eastern sportswriters claimed football teams on the West Coast did not play well enough to justify the long, round-trip train ride. From then until 1921, only five football games had been included in the Tournament of Roses events, and two of those contests involved military teams. No games were scheduled pitting West Coast teams against the powerhouses from the East or Midwest. Nineteen years later, the pleasant weather conditions in Pasadena, contrasted to the snow and ice in the Midwest, had tempted the powerful and unbeaten Ohio State Buckeyes to venture westward to play the California Bears at the Arroyo Seco Stadium. It had been just one year ago, to the amazement of easterners and the delight of sports fans in the west, the California Bears and their star player, Brick Muller, had ripped apart the once proud Buckeyes 28 to 0.

Now, newspapers back east were predicting the mighty Lions of Penn State would inflict havoc on Gus Henderson's USC Trojans and avenge the indignity suffered by an Ohio State team that apparently wasn't as good as most had estimated.

*   *   *

After catching a few hours sleep following several late night visits to New Years Eve parties at various men's and women's fraternity parties along "The Row," Bud picked-up Dawn at her home before daybreak. They drove to Pasadena, found a parking place near Colorado Avenue, and secured a spot along the curb to watch the spectacular floats parade down Colorado Boulevard. A floral Viking ship with shields and oars, a blossom-covered goose that measured over ten car lengths, and a flower bedecked king's harem with pretty girls waving to parade watchers were some of the creative ideas decorating the newly motorized floats. After the USC marching band strutted past playing, "Fight On," the Trojan fight song written this semester by Bud's dental student friend, Milo Sweet, they hurried back to Dawn's Packard. Bud drove between the parade route and the newly built Rose Bowl while she relaxed and enjoyed the sun on her face. Their picnic basket was riding on the floor of the back seat. The traffic noise, as well as the roar of the big twin-six engine, made conversation difficult, but contented smiles were frequently exchanged.

She closed her eyes for a short nap, and he began reflecting back on their first New Years Eve celebration together. A damp chill in the air had been reminiscent of beach parties on cold, wintry nights in Oxnard and made Bud happy to slip on his dark-blue wool suit-coat. Wearing a necktie was not as pleasant. The invitation to the Dee Gee New Year's Eve Dance specified the dress to be formal, which meant the guys would be warm while the bare shouldered girls in their light-weight dresses would be shivering. The young men's ability to keep their dates comfortable depended upon how affectionate the couple had become. He walked the short distance to the Dee Gee house with some other boys who had received invitations to the same party. Other men's fraternity members joined them along the way. Musical numbers from years past were heard from other women's fraternity houses where parties were just getting underway.

Dawn greeted him at the door wearing a marine blue strapless dress that showed off her pretty shoulders and arms.

"You have any room left for me on your dance card?" he asked.

"I might find a spot or two," she replied. She showed him her dance card. "What do you know? Your name is on the very top. I wonder how that happened."

A three-piece band played in one corner of the dining hall converted into dance floor. Parties they had previously attended were informal, which he thought was his preference. The feel of his hand on her bare back as they did the two-step to "Who's Sorry Now?" caused him to reconsider his position. Later in the evening, looking at other men's hands in the same spot on Dawn's back was not as pleasant. His reaction seemed justified when she appeared annoyed at some of the pretty DeeGees he twirled around the dance floor.

When they were dancing the last dance, he'd whispered in her ear, "You're the prettiest girl here."

She had responded, "Of course you're right, but it's still nice to hear."

"And also the most modest," he added.

The highlight of the evening was the lingering kiss they had shared as 1922 turned into 1923.

Dawn interrupted Bud's day dream. "Do you think we'll win today?"

"It's pretty hard to figure since we don't play any common opponents."

They planned to arrive early for a picnic lunch before the game and were surprised at how many other fans had the same idea. Football games at Bovard Field were always colorful and exciting, but they hadn't anticipated the exhilarating atmosphere surrounding this event.

She spread out the blanket on a green patch of lawn and asked, "Why do they call it the Rose Bowl when it's shaped more like a horseshoe?"

"I believe they will eventually complete the circle. I heard the city fathers want to pattern it after the Yale Bowl."

Relaxing in the sun and munching on Mama Smith's fried chicken, they observed men and women of all ages dressed in cardinal-and-gold attire, while others walked past carrying Penn State pennants.

*　　*　　*

From Bud and Dawn's vantage point in the USC student section, it soon became apparent the Penn State Lions were no more a match for USC than Ohio State had been for California one year ago. Left Guard, Leo Callard, big Swede Anderson, and other members of the Trojan line tackled Penn State's Lions before they could reach the line of scrimmage and opened large holes for Bullet Baker and Otto Anderson to run through when USC was on offense. Late in the game, Penn State's only sustained drive stalled on the Trojan twenty-five yard line, and the Lions had to drop kick the ball through the goal posts for three points.

Gloomy Gus Henderson was all smiles as he sent in the reserves to finish the game. 14 to 3 was not as humiliating as Ohio State's collapse last year, but Henderson was not known to run up the score once the game was won.

Dawn watched disappointed Penn State fans heading for the exits and remarked, "I feel sorry for them traveling so far and then getting beat so bad."

"Let's hope the rest of their stay in California was more enjoyable," Bud replied.

Chapter 21

April 1923

The best track team in California would be determined at the AAU Track Meet at Redlands today. Dean Cromwell's USC Trojan squad had conquered every foe and boasted some athletes many thought would represent America in the 1924 Olympics to be held in Paris, France. The only team to beat them this year was the USC Freshman in a practice meet at Bovard Field. The varsity was determined not to suffer that humiliation again. After beating the Trojan Varsity the frosh had gone on to whip San Fernando 86 to 27, Hollywood High 84 to 29, LA High 83 to 30, and a powerful Polytechnic squad 82 to 30. It was no surprise that no high school team could match up to the best former high school athletes from schools all around the country.

The upperclassmen boasted one of the fastest men in the state in sprinter, Yale Martz. Otto Anderson had beaten the best hurdlers in California, and their star weight man, Norman "Swede" Anderson, had prevailed over everyone he faced, with the exception of freshman Bud Houser. The varsity also figured that Corey would win the high jump, Emmons the pole vault and their sprinters would likely take first in the mile relay.

In contrast to the Varsity's resolve to undo their only loss, the freshman had whipped these upperclassmen once and intended to prove that it was no fluke. Wilson was the favorite in the broad jump, and Niersback and Smith should win second and third place medals in the 880. Mueller usually ran like a demon in both the high hurdles and could beat anyone if he ran his best race, while Lowe and Starry figured to take second and third in the sprints. Figure Bud's first place medals in the shot and discus, and the meet should be very close. The freshmen team's one disadvantage was the man who had the best chance to defeat Otto Anderson in both the high and low hurdles, Leighton "never say" Dye, was sick and could not compete.

Neither the Trojans nor Trobabes could afford many slip-ups with a powerful Occidental squad breathing down their necks. Ellsworth from Oxy was favored to win the 880, Carter should prevail in the mile, and Bud's old high school buddy, Cliff Argue, would give Yale Martz all he could handle in the sprints. The Oxy mile-relay team would also be difficult to beat. Add in a few other seconds and thirds, and Occidental could pull an upset. It promised to be an interesting afternoon.

Bud watched freshman teammate, Wilson, win the broad jump and Niersback barely get edged out by Occidental's Ellsworth in the 880 before going over to the discus ring. After his first toss went at least twelve feet beyond what anyone else at the meet would be able to manage, he was only competing against his own distances.

Once he'd won first place in the discus, he had some time before the shot put competition, and went to watch Cliff Argue line up against Yale Martz in the 100 yard dash. A freshman standing next to him said that Martz had only beat Argue by about a foot in the 200, and Corey had edged Argue out in the high jump when Argue barely clipped the bar on his last attempt. Bud found himself torn between rooting for his school or his old friend.

Yale Martz and Cliff Argue took off simultaneously and battled all the way down the track with neither able to pull into the lead. They continued matching each other step for step until they crossed the finish line.

"Who won?" a voice from the crowd cried out.

No one knew until they heard on the loud speaker, "Ladies and gentlemen, Yale Martz and Cliff Argue finished the 100-yard dash with identical times of nine point nine seconds. The official at the finish line has ruled that Martz leaned across the finish just a few inches ahead of Argue. The official results of the finals in the 100 yard dash are Martz of USC first, Argue of Occidental second, Anderson of USC third, and Lowe of the USC Freshmen fourth."

Bud was happy for Yale but felt sick watching his old friend with his head down in defeat. With just a little luck, Cliff could have won three first-place medals today. Before he could go over to provide encouragement, the loudspeaker announced the beginning of the shot put event.

It all came down to this last event. If the varsity could pull an upset and win a first- place medal in the shot put, they would edge out the USC Frosh and win the track meet. If Bud Houser and Norman "Swede" Anderson each performed at their highest level, the Trojans would have to accept another defeat by their younger classmates, and this time it would be official. Alma Richards of the LAAC was only a few feet behind Bud and Swede's best marks.

Bud had been noticing several weight men copying his crouch and accelerating spin before pushing the shot put, so he wasn't surprised when Thomas of the freshman team rode this strategy to a 41 foot 2 inch toss on his first attempt. Swede Anderson went next and landed his toss at 45 feet 4 inches, a personal best for him. Alma Richards had a disappointing 39 foot eleven inches, and it was time for Bud to do what he did best. His crouch was low and the spin and toss felt like so many times before, but the 16-pound ball landed only 44 feet seven inches out. He knew he had to do better to win this event.

On Swede's third toss, the shot put landed at 45 feet 8 and 1/2 inches, bettering his earlier toss by over 4 inches.

"Nice throw, Swede," Bud said as he stepped up to the ring.

Bud had been in this position so many times it was becoming repetitive. He crouched lower, spun faster, and pushed harder than his two earlier tosses. He watched the metal ball fly through the air and land in the grass further than either of his previous tries, but still a few inches short of the big Swede's final throw.

The varsity track and field men who had gathered to watch this deciding event erupted in a loud cheer as they realized they had finally prevailed over their younger counterparts.

Bud's initial reaction was disbelief. He had done everything the same way as before and had no idea why his distance was so far short of his best. He saw Cliff Argue's face among the crowd and walked over to him.

"Rough day, old buddy," Cliff greeted.

"I saw you run the hundred. I thought you had Yale beat."

"Did you see our time? We both have to run faster than that to have any chance of qualifying for the 1924 Olympics. Charlie Paddock has been running nine point six regularly."

"That's strange. The way you two were battling, I would think you would have run your best times."

"You'd think so."

"It was the same with me, Cliff. I knew Swede had performed at his top level, and I needed my best to win. I just don't know what happened." Bud saw Dawn and his sister, Martha, waving at them from the front row of the bleachers. "Come with me," he said. "I want you to meet the love of my life."

"Congratulations, Bud," Dawn said as they approached.

"For what?" Bud asked.

"For winning the discus and taking second in the shot put."

"He's never happy unless he wins everything," Martha said. "That's one of the reasons he's so hard to beat."

"Cliff, you know my sister and her husband, Walter, this is Dr. Christopher Smith, Cora Smith and their daughter, Dawn."

After shaking hands with the men and greeting the women, Cliff turned to Dawn. "It seems like I've heard your name somewhere before."

"You might know my cousin, Ray Wilhite."

Cliff's face lit up with its first smile since his disappointing defeats. He grinned at Bud and said, "Yes, I believe I remember Ray mentioning your name."

Dr. Smith rose to his feet. "Walter and I have been talking about the disappointments you two faced today and would like to offer a suggestion or two."

Martha smiled indulgently at her husband, and then turned to the ladies, "Would you like to get some lemonade?"

When the men were alone, Dr. Smith turned to Walter and said, "Why don't you tell them our observations?"

Walter chuckled, "You boys have to remember we're just two old geezers who can't perform like you so we have to put in our two cents."

"Our advice is probably worth less than what you're paying for it," Dr. Smith added.

"Go ahead," Cliff urged.

"No one is always going to perform at their peak level, in any sport," Walter continued. "Cliff, if the best hundred you've run is 9.8, keep working until to get your time down to 9.6. Bud, if you best shot put is 50 feet, try to regularly toss it 52 or 53 feet. Never be satisfied with the best you've done before."

Dr. Smith added, "What we're saying is, never assume that on any given day you're going to be better than the guy you're competing against. Give yourself some margin for error so that if you have an off day, you will still win."

Cliff folded his arms and leaned back against the seat behind him. "I'll tell you gentlemen this. The next time I compete against Yale Martz, he's going to have to run a lot faster than he did today if he wants to beat me again."

Walter elbowed Dr. Smith and said, "I think he's trying to humor us."

"Not really," Bud remarked. "Cliff and I knew we had to get better, but it never hurts to enforce that idea. You two have certainly proved you know what it takes to succeed."

Dr. Smith added, "You two have youth on your side. I know it's not too comforting right now, but the guys that beat you today are a few years older."

When the ladies returned, Martha and Cora each held two lemonades while Dawn was carefully balancing three.

Over the loud speaker they all heard, "May I have your attention? Here again are the final team scores for today; USC Varsity forty-six and one-half points; USC Frosh forty-two points; Occidental thirty-nine points."

"Yeah, yeah, we heard you the first time," Cliff grumbled.

Chapter 22

August 29, 1923

The cool Los Angeles air was always a welcome change from the intense heat of the San Joaquin Valley. Bud stepped off the bus at the Los Angeles train depot and immediately saw Dawn's smiling face. He ran to her, picked her up in his arms, and twirled her around. He determined that two months was too long for them to be apart. While working his summer job at Lake Shore Warehouse in Corcoran, the couple had exchanged letters several times a week, which only increased their longing to be together.

"I'm not going to let you out of my sight for the next two days," he promised.

"And then you're off to Chicago to beat everyone in the country again."

"But this time I'll only be gone for a week."

"Did you get all the newspaper clippings I sent to you?"

"I did. It seems a lot of local reporters think I only have to show up and they'll hand me two first place medals. Do they know how many guys twice my size want to prove them wrong?"

"I guess they have a lot of confidence in you. You came pretty close last year and you're setting better marks now."

"The Olympic Games are only a year off; the competition will be much tougher. Anyway, let's forget about track. During these next couple of days, I intend to make up for lost time with you. I'm sure you have tons of things planned."

"Spending some time alone with you tops the list."

*　　　*　　　*

September 3

Bud sat alongside athletes he'd participated against and stared out the hotel's dining room window at the continuing rain. His mind went back to Chicago's Stagg Field two days ago. The reports in Chicago newspapers about this being a freak storm for this time of year were of no help to the sprinters he had watched sloshing down the track before the field events began. Later he observed the frustration of those participating in the high jump and the struggles the distance men faced in the mile run. It was doubtful if many records would fall in this weather.

The mud in the shot put ring had felt like a water drenched sponge under his feet and the 16 pound ball was slippery. A short time later, he found conditions for throwing the discus even worse. He could feel the saucer sliding from his hands on the first two tries before finally getting a nice toss on his final attempt.

In contrast to the miserable conditions at Stagg Field, the Amateur Athletic Union could not have chosen a more elegant spot than the Gold Room of Chicago's Congress Hotel for the awards dinner. He wished he could blame the torrential rain for his poor performance in the shot put and discus rings, but the other contestants had to labor under the same conditions.

After he had polished off a salad, T-bone steak, and a dessert that he enjoyed without knowing what he was eating, the awards presentations began. Bud forced a smile and applauded when Wanzer from the New York Athletic Club picked up the first-place medal in the shot-put and again when Eastman from the Boston Athletic Club accepted the second-place medal. He finally made his way up to the podium to accept third-place. The worst part about taking third was he had set much better marks in track meets at USC's Bovard Field.

The discus medal presentation was different only in the names of the first and second-place winners. Lieb of the Illinois Athletic Club won first-place, Gus Pope, also of the Illinois Athletic Club took second, and Bud again picked up the third-place medal. Why, he wondered, did he get a larger ovation from the crowd than the people who had beaten him? Was it because he was the only athlete to win two medals, or perhaps because he was younger? Maybe it was because the other medal winners were several inches taller and fifty to a hundred pounds heavier. Was his comparatively small stature the reason newspapers around the nation gave him more ink than all these others? A guy built like a sprinter competing in the weight events? This reasoning provided no comfort. Being the best for his age and size had never been his goal.

The only numbers he was interested in were the 23 inches short he'd been in losing the discuss and the extra foot and a half his shot put needed to travel to have taken first-place. Maybe building up his strength with hard labor was not as effective as he had thought. Next year, whether working in Corcoran or not, he would be giving a lot more time to practicing his events. Remembering the words of Dr. Smith and Walter Conklin, he decided to make whatever sacrifices were needed to add a few feet to his target distances in both events. Who knew how much better some of the weight men in Europe might be, or what kind of weather he would have to face? That is, if he even qualified to go to the Olympics. He was convinced he needed to improve in at least one of his events to make this dream become a reality.

As much as he enjoyed football, he didn't see how he could be on the team next year while keeping up his grades in dental school and adding the required distance in his two field events. Something would have to go.

*   *   *

As the Los Angeles Express rolled down the rails back through Missouri, Bud looked at cornfields and farmhouses much like the ones he remembered from his boyhood. Memories came flooding back of how huge his older brothers had seemed and how proud he always felt when he wrestled them to the floor. Even then he had known they were letting him win. When the time came for the Olympic trials, everyone was going to be desperately trying to prevent him from winning. He had come a long way, but still had a lot of distance to cover.

Whitened fields flashing by his window gradually changed to mountain cabins and pine trees as the locomotive pulling the train huffed and puffed up an incline. Watching a laughing couple on horseback riding along a picturesque stream, he felt lonely for Dawn. Realistically, it would no doubt be impossible to have her at Harvard Stadium next year, cheering him on to win the right to represent his country in the Olympics. The main thing was for her to be in the stadium in Paris as he battled to beat men almost twice his size. To protect her reputation from talk about unmarried lovers traveling together, he decided he would ask his sister, Martha, to accompany them.

Chapter 23

The annual trek to San Francisco was becoming a tradition for USC students and alumni. On alternate years they would travel to watch the football team play Stanford at Palo Alto, or their old nemesis, the California Bears at Berkeley. Both men's and women's fraternities along Fraternity Row were making the most of it. Many students already lived on or near 28th Street, far away from the guidance of their parents, but traveling to another city was somehow more provocative. Students could travel by train, bus, automobile, or boat. Men's and women's fraternity house managers had rented rooms in nice hotels and planned to pile enough Trojans into each room to reduce the individual cost. Bud had been trying to figure out how his budget would permit the bus or train ride until a recent evening at Dr. and Mama Smith's house.

Dawn had picked him up at the Sigma Chi house, supposedly to go to the movie Stagecoach and then remembered she had not brought a sweater. Since her parents' house on Pico Boulevard was only ten minutes from the campus, this presented no major problem. The first people Bud saw as he walked into the large living room were his track buddy, Leighton Dye, and Leighton's girlfriend, Eleanor. Before he could figure out why they were there, he was surrounded by several Sigma Chi brothers, most of Dawn's Dee Gee sisters and some men from the track team. Dawn grinned at him all through the singing of *Happy*

Birthday. He had no doubt who had been the mastermind of this sweet deception.

Mama Smith had prepared a table with all sorts of goodies and, while there was not much bare floor for dancing, many did what they called *cutting a rug.* A few of Bud's fraternity brothers and track team members already knew the Dee Gees, however, one or two new romances appeared to be budding.

When it was time for Bud to cut his birthday cake, Dr. Smith handed him an envelope and apologized for not having wrapped his gift.

Later, Dawn watched over his shoulder as he tore open the envelope. Inside were two tickets from Los Angeles to San Francisco on the S.S. Yale of the Yale-Harvard Cruise Line. The City of Oxnard had financed a trip to Chicago for his first AAU track meet, and the LA Athletic Club had paid for another, but he had never received a gift of this magnitude. He had heard about the steamship liner that transported students, players, and faculty to the football games, but never thought he would be able to afford traveling in this manner. He turned to Dr. and Mrs. Smith. "I don't know what to say. This is just overwhelming."

Dr. Smith smiled and put his arm around his wife. "It was our pleasure."

When Bud and Dawn were alone, he showed her where one ticket read Stateroom 107 and the other Stateroom 109. "It looks like our rooms are only two doors apart."

"I understand they're next to each other," she corrected. "108 should be across the hall."

"How did you swing that?"

"It wasn't easy. Of course the Dee Gee house-mother is right across the hall. Dad trusts us, but he always has been a little over-protective."

"You think he's over-protective? Wait until we have a little girl. I won't even let her date until she's thirty."

*   *   *

Well-to-do alumni far outnumbered students boarding the S.S. Yale at Los Angeles Harbor; some were old enough to be Bud and Dawn's grandparents. Age certainly had not detracted from the excitement of the moment nor the desire to whip Leland Stanford University this coming Saturday. Old Trojans wore the school colors and second-guessed how Gus Henderson, with the right strategy, could have defeated the University of Washington at Seattle last week. Few old-timers gave Gus credit for the USC Varsity outscoring opponents 74 to 14 up until last week's game. Popular opinion reflected that, in order to return to the Rose Bowl, we would have to win this week, whip our old tormentors, the California Bears, at the newly built Los Angeles Memorial Coliseum, and then conclude by defeating Arizona and Idaho. Even that scenario wouldn't assure the Trojans a New Years game in Pasadena unless someone beat the University of Washington Huskies.

Bud remembered, during his younger years, sitting on the beach and watching these magnificent ships traveling up and down the coast. He never dreamed he would one day be on board one of them. He had heard that the Harvard and Yale had been stripped of their luxurious appointments during wartime and had transported hundreds of thousands of the victors in the great world war. Now he admired glistening paint and gleaming brass accompanying the furnishing of one of the country's great floating hotels.

Unencumbered by luggage, the two raced each other to Staterooms 107 and 109. Prior descriptions of the luxury rooms lessoned their surprise, but not their excitement. Her suitcase had already been placed next to a small closet. She rushed over to the window and pulled back the curtain. All that greeted her was an old wooden dock and a warehouse behind it.

"Nice room, but not much of a view," Bud observed.

"You're being silly. On this side of the ship we'll get to see the coastline on the way to San Francisco. Look, they even have a radio. She glanced at the upper and lower berths for a few seconds before saying, "Let's go look at your room."

As expected, his room was a replica of hers, only with the beds and furnishings reversed.

"Meet you back in the hall in three minutes," she called as she raced back out the door.

*   *   *

Signs along the deck read, *"The Trojans go up to down the Indians, Trojans will strut their stuff at Stanford. Welcome Trojan students and fans."* Working their way from aft to forward, they first entered the smoking room filled with large comfortable chairs, free-standing ashtrays, and a large radio. The smell of stale cigarette smoke drove them quickly back into the fresh sea air on the deck. The giant ship began slowly edging away from its berth, and they leaned over the rail and watched until there was about a mile of blue ocean between them and the shoreline.

She crossed her arms with her hands gripping her shoulders. "Wow, it's colder out here. Let's see the rest of the ship. There must be better places than the smoking room."

Like two inquisitive children they strolled in and out of a small library, a game room with poker tables and roulette wheel, a ballroom with floors polished to a mirror-like finish and a dining hall bigger than the dining room at the Los Angeles Biltmore Hotel. A quick peek into the wheel room left them with only the observation lounge on the front of the ship still to explore.

Once inside, they found a couple of comfortable chairs and watched the bow of the ship plow through the water.

"I believe we saved the best for last," he said. "Your dad is really a great guy giving me a gift like this."

"I'm just glad you chose me to share it with."

"It was a tough decision, but once I narrowed it down to the DeeGees you seemed like the best choice."

*   *   *

The cover of the dinner menu for their first night aboard ship showed two red, white, and blue ships sailing side by side. Inside were pictures of Coach Gus Henderson and Johnny Hawkins, captain of the Trojan football team, along with the selection of food to be served.

"Do you think you'll be able to eat all this?" he asked.

"Oh gee, I'm sure going to try."

In spite of her promise, Dawn ate just a small amount of the Sardine Canape, a few spoonfuls of the Pismo Clam Chowder, about half of what the menu called "*Cardinal T Bone steak*," most of her banana fritters, completely ignored her boiled potatoes, and polished off her "*Varsity Salad.*"

While cleaning each plate set before him, Bud hadn't noticed how his companion had conserved her appetite. When they brought out dishes piled high with chocolate covered ice cream along with assorted cakes, he leaned back in his chair and asked, "Do you think we have room for dessert?"

"No problem," she answered as she took a sizeable bite of ice cream.

Suddenly the rhythmic sounds of loud drums came floating across the dining room. Students and alumni leaped to their feet as trombones, cornets, and a tuba blared out the song that now represented the spirit of Troy, "*Fight On.*" Decked out in full cardinal-and-gold uniform, twelve selected members of the Trojan band continued the loud music while marching past the cheering diners and up to the platform. One of the Trojan yell leaders appeared and led the assembled fans in cheering and singing. After the crowd had been whipped into a frenzy of school spirit, the young man asked for everyone to listen to an announcement he had to make. "I would like to introduce a member of the Trojan band." He walked over and pulled one of the trombone players from among the group. "Ladies and gentlemen, I would like to introduce you to Al Wesson. This is his senior year and last year with the Trojan band. He is leaving us with something that I predict will live on after all of us are gone. If you will look under the tablecloth in front of you, you'll find the words and music to a beautiful song Al has written. While you're doing that, the band will play the music so that when we sing it, you will all know the tune.

To everyone's surprise, the melody the band played sounded more like a hymn than an inspiring fight song.

"Okay, now that you know the tune, let's put the words with it," the yell leader announced.

People began haltingly at first and then sang more loudly as they became familiar with the words of "*All hail to Southern California.*"

Strong men and decorous ladies tried to stifle their emotions as the sweet music poured across the room. Where "*Fight On,*" written just last year, inspired excitement, Al Wesson's school hymn left few dry eyes throughout the crowd of students and alumni and faculty.

On their way back to their staterooms, Bud said, "Wow! What an exciting evening! I can't believe with all the food we had you could still finish your dessert. I'm completely stuffed, and I weigh at least 70 pounds more than you."

She reached into her purse and pulled out a small green ticket. On it was printed her weight and fortune.

"You have a quiet, slow, but rather forceful nature," he read. "Oh look, you should get your penny back; it got your weight wrong, too. A little girl like you couldn't weigh 114 pounds."

She snatched the card back. "Muscle weighs more than fat, and I am very quiet and demure."

"Of course you are, sweetheart."

Chapter 24

As soon as Bud and Dawn climbed off the Trojan rooter bus that had met them at the dock, they saw several Trojan Knights, recognizable by their cardinal vee-necked sweaters and white shirts. One of the Knights greeted them carrying a list of men's and women's fraternities and their room numbers. The Saint Francis Hotel was not completely unaware that there would be additional guests occupying selected rooms, but the student leaders didn't want to flaunt this minor violation. A room for twelve dollars a night was beyond the budget of most students, but dividing the cost of each room five or six ways provided affordable accommodations.

Like most people on campus, the young man knew Bud Houser and his girlfriend, Dawn, and he told them where to find the rooms Sigma Chi and DeeGee had reserved.

The turn of the century lobby of the Saint Francis Hotel boasted sumptuous columns of filigree and marble along with plush carpeting and ornately upholstered chairs and couches. Most of the people milling around or waiting in line at the front desk were wearing Trojan colors. From Bud and Dawn's vantage point it appeared Trojan fans had taken over the town. It only took the first clang of the bell on a cable car going up Powell Street to inspire Bud's announcement of his love for San Francisco.

"This is a great place to watch for celebrities," Dawn whispered. "Even kings and presidents have stayed here."

They had been advised to take their luggage straight to their rooms without checking in at the front desk. Before heading for the elevator, they agreed to meet at the lobby in

15 minutes. The train bound for Stanford Stadium in Palo Alto would be leaving the station in just over an hour, so they had little time to spare. Seeing the sights in San Francisco would be reserved for tonight.

*   *   *

Trees along the walk from the train to the stadium provided an array of fall colors that would be hard to find in Southern California. The clear blue sky and cool Northern California air had set up a perfect day for football. All this beauty would go unappreciated if the Trojan Varsity didn't whip Stanford this afternoon.

When they reached their seats in the USC student section, Bud said, "I'll go back in the tunnel and grab us some hot dogs and cold drinks."

"Just one hot dog for me," Dawn said.

Bud returned with only two hot dogs and two drinks.

"Did you lose your appetite?" she asked.

"Forty cents for two hot dogs and two orange drinks; I hope the Coliseum doesn't charge those prices."

They looked around at other students removing sandwiches from brown paper bags.

"Live and learn," she remarked.

"I've heard San Francisco's Chinatown has good food at reasonable prices," he said.

"Let's hope so."

Against Cal Tech, Pomona, and Nevada, the graduation of guards Callard and Dougher and tackles Freeman and Galloway had hardly been noticed. Students and alumni hoped Coach Henderson had bolstered the line enough to prevent another humiliating loss like the one at Seattle last week. Accompanied by loud cheering from the local crowd and groans from the visiting USC rooting section, Stanford took the opening kickoff and marched the length of the field for a touchdown. They drop-kicked the extra point for a quick 7 to 0 lead, and USC fans settled back for a long afternoon.

The Trojans couldn't move the ball on their first possession and had to surrender it back to Stanford. From that point on defensive play dominated. With just a couple minutes left in the first half, neither team had been able add any score, and the cardinal and gold fans were getting impatient. The Trojans finally began moving the ball down the field, and with just a few seconds left in the half, the Trojans surprised Stanford on an end around, and Bud's Sigma Chi buddy, Ben Gerpheide, took the ball down the sideline for a score. Bullet Baker drop-kicked the extra point, and the teams left the field tied, 7 to 7.

As the bands marched out on the field for the halftime ceremonies, Dawn asked, "Do you wish you were playing today?"

"More than you know."

She squeezed his hand. "I hope you're not giving-up something you want to do because of me?"

He crossed his arms and became silent.

"I want you to be happy. If playing football and baseball is what you want most, I'll support your decision. You can still play your junior and senior years."

"It is tempting, but I'm trying to do what I think is best. You know I didn't have any formal schooling until I was almost twelve years old. Getting good grades in high school was harder for me than for some others. I know I can't keep up my grades in dental school and play all of the sports, and I don't want to be broke when I'm thirty-five years old. If I can win the Olympics and graduate from dental school, I believe we will have a better life because of it."

She suddenly grinned. "We will have a better life? Is it my imagination, or did I hear a marriage proposal just now?"

"It must have been your imagination."

She punched him on the arm, but received no response, as he doubled his fist at another line plunge by the Trojans that yielded no gain.

With just a few minutes left in the game, it appeared to both rooting sections that USC and Stanford would have to settle for a 7 to 7 tie. Then suddenly Trojan fans leaped to their feet screaming their lungs out as, out of the mass of humanity, Roy "Bullet" Baker broke loose and raced down the field toward the Stanford goal line.

The band, yell leaders, and song girls were still down on the field entertaining the celebrating Trojan fans long after the Stanford rooters had left the stadium.

*   *   *

Holding hands and walking along Fisherman's Wharf, Dawn said, "It's sure more fun seeing the town after we've won the game."

"You probably don't know this about me, but I've always preferred winning."

"Gosh, I'm glad you told me."

"That was a pretty nice dinner we had for only 60 cents," Bud remarked.

"Who would have believed we'd find a great restaurant down an alley in Chinatown?"

"I would never have thought to ask at the front desk for recommendations."

"You're welcome," she said.

He laughed. "Dawn, I think this weekend has been the most fun I've ever had."

She squeezed his arm a little tighter, and then looked across the black water. "What are those lights out there?"

"That's Alcatraz Island."

"They have homes on the island?"

"It's mostly a bird sanctuary, but I believe the lights are from a small military prison."

"In that case, I don't want to go there."

Bud held Dawn closely during the chilly cable-car ride from Fisherman's Wharf to the front entrance of the hotel.

"We have to come back here again," Dawn said.

*　　*　　*

Anyone who walked down the fifth floor of the Saint Francis Hotel at eleven o'clock Saturday night might think it had turned into a comic lover's lane. Five Dee Gee rooms and only one housemother created a silent-movie type of scenario. Couples were maneuvering to get in one more goodnight kiss while the housemother was running from door to door trying to shew her flock safely into their rooms.

When they reached her hotel room door, Dawn gave Bud a quick peck on the lips and said, "Let's save it for the boat trip home."

"Save what?"

She doubled up her fist, but he quickly skipped out of the way.

"Goodnight Bud, I had a wonderful time."

"I hope I'll hear you say the same words tomorrow night."

Apparently unaffected by her puzzled frown, he patted her cheek, turned and walked down the hall.

Chapter 25

Standing on the starboard deck, Bud and Dawn watched the beaches and mountains of Northern and Central California slip by. It seemed that eating was the primary activity aboard the S.S. Yale with breakfast being followed by a mid-morning snack, followed by lunch, after which an assortment of fruits, pastries and nuts lined tables in both the main dining room and observation lounge.

Leaning on the ship's railing Bud said, "I don't think I'll eat again for a week."

"I'll remind you of that at dinner tonight," Dawn replied. "I don't see how this weekend could have been more perfect."

Again, Bud had that faraway look in his eyes that puzzled her.

"What?" she inquired.

"I didn't say anything."

"It's what you're not saying that worries me."

"Are you looking forward to the victory celebration tonight?" he asked.

"It's better than hearing all of the second guessing when our team loses."

"You've noticed that, too. The biggest complainers seem to be people who have never competed in sports."

"So you won't do that when you get to be an alumni?"

He thought for a few seconds and then said, "No guarantees. I do love to win."

"I remember you telling Dad we should have passed more in the Washington State game last year."

He began a long explanation of why he thought football teams should be passing more and not just trying to run over people.

When he paused with his dissertation, she yawned and said, "It's been such a non-stop weekend, I think I'll take a nap before dinner."

"Maybe I'll go back up to the observation lounge. I'll knock on your door about 15 minutes before dinner."

"Save your appetite," she warned.

Dawn rested on her lower berth but couldn't sleep. Something about the way Bud had been acting made her restless. She tried to remember all that had happened the last few days to see if she could get a clue to his strange behavior. Could she have done something to make him angry? Out of the blue, a horrible thought entered her mind. "He's going to break up with me." From the first time they'd met, she'd assumed they would always be together. Her self assurance, which never in her life had been a problem, took a sudden dive. At L.A. High School, she had always had her pick of boys to date. The thought of someone breaking up with her had never crossed her mind. He had shared with her that he'd always been too busy working or competing in sports to date anyone. "Why should someone who could have any girl he chose want to settle down with the first girl he had dated?" She felt sick to her stomach.

Bud wandered around the decks practicing what he wanted to say to Dawn. No matter how many times he reviewed it, it never sounded right. Tonight after dinner, he would just say it the best way he could and hope her response was positive.

*   *   *

Shortly before the ship's scheduled time for dinner, she heard a soft knock on her door. She took one last look in the mirror to see if the cold washrags had taken away the swelling in her eyes. She smoothed her navy-blue dress, picked up her gray wool flannel coat and opened the door. His face looked so solemn she almost burst into tears. This was supposed to be a happy occasion, how could it end this way?

"You look beautiful," he said.

She mumbled, "Thank you."

"You better let me help you into your coat. It's cold out on the deck."

"I can just put it over my shoulders."

They walked silently into the dining room, said only a few words during dinner, and clapped politely as the band played the songs that had stirred up so much excitement two nights before.

After dinner, most of the alumni headed straight for their staterooms, leaving Bud and Dawn and a few other couples wandering the decks and finding the best and most isolated spots to gaze at shafts of moonlight stretching out across the black rippling water.

She decided to let him say the first words and waited several seconds before she heard him clear his throat to speak. She tuned her face away, bit her lip and blinked her eyes several times. When she finally turned back toward him, she saw a small box in his hand.

"Dawn, honey, I'm not any good at things like this, and frankly, I'm scared to death. He opened the box and showed her a gold band with a small diamond. I know this isn't much, but it's all I can afford right now. Anyway, I guess the only words I know to say are I love you very much and I want to spend the rest of my life with you. So, will you to marry me?"

She buried her face against his chest and left it there for several seconds.

"You don't have to give me an answer right now if you want to think about it for a while."

Without looking up she asked, "Haven't you noticed? I've been in love with you since the first night we met."

He pushed her back so he could see her face. "Does that mean yes?"

106

"Yes! You big crazy guy, that means yes!"

He took a deep breath and blew it out slowly. She lifted her hand and he gently slipped the ring on her finger.

She looked down at the shiny gold band with its tiny diamond and knew it was the most beautiful ring she had ever seen. Putting her right hand behind his head, she grinned mischievously. "As wonderful as this evening has already been, are we going to waste this moon just talking?"

Later, outside of Dawn's stateroom, Bud kissed her softly on the lips and whispered, "One of these days I won't have to say goodnight at your door."

Chapter 26

As much as Bud enjoyed living in the Sigma Chi house, he learned early on that it was not the place to study, especially for one determined to get a degree in dentistry. Etched in his mind was the panic he felt last year when the letter arrived from Dean Lewis E. Ford. He knew it only took one bad semester and he was out. When he tore open the envelope, to his relief he read, " *I wish to extend to you my congratulations.*" Along with the letter was his certificate of promotion to the sophomore class.

Rather than going directly into the school library this evening, he parked himself on a bench under a young oak tree. As a child, finding alone-time had been as easy as going out to the barn and climbing into the hayloft. Now, being some place where he could review his progress and plan the next steps of his life took some effort. Slipping a ring on Dawn's finger had assured him of spending his future with the girl he loved. Graduating from dental school would take some hard work, but he had no doubt he would also reach that goal. Qualifying for the 1924 Olympic Team was the major hurtle in front of him. Setting world's records in intercollegiate track meets was not going to get the job done. During his first year of college, he hadn't won when it counted. He had to become the best weight man in the nation, whether he participated in the mud or on dry ground. His worst tosses in the shot put and discus had to be better than the best marks of his competition. It would be nice if he had until his senior year to reach those goals, but he only had his sophomore year of competition before the Olympic tryouts would be held. Another incentive to make the

Olympic team was Dawn's guarantee that if he went to Paris, she would go with him. By now, he knew that when his future bride was determined to do something, heaven help those who stood in her way.

As he watched dusk turn to darkness and the lights come on in the library, he wondered what it would be like to honeymoon with his beautiful fiancée in Paris. That thought was more stimulating than he had anticipated, and he quickly picked up his books and hurried into the library. He might have to study late into this Thursday night since there would be little chance to study over the busy weekend he and Dawn had planned.

*   *   *

Walking down the tunnel toward the USC rooting section, Dawn looked and acted considerably different than the feisty young lady he had watched last night help her Pico Avenue Christian Church win their second straight YMCA Sunday school basketball championship. Today she wore a medium-length cardinal skirt, gold sweater, with white and brown saddle shoes and white socks. Last night her uniform consisted of a navy-blue short skirt with long navy-blue stockings and a vee-neck pullover blouse with a large white letter S, for Saints, on the front. She had worn regulation black tennis shoes of the kind he had never before seen on girls. Walking behind her down the tunnel, there was no hint that this demure young coed was the five-foot two inch tiger that aggressively dove and scrambled after loose basketballs, dribbled around and past the Congregational Church girls, shot baskets with deadly accuracy, and argued with the referee when he called fouls on her for charging-with-the-ball. "Yeah, she's a little saint, alright," he thought.

As they reached their seats, she asked, "Why are we so far away from the field?"

"The Coliseum was built for the 1924 Olympics. The track around the field pushes the seats quite a bit further back."

"But the Olympics are in Paris."

"The Coliseum Committee was disappointed, but they're pretty sure they'll get the games here in 1928 or 1932."

She looked around at the sparse crowd between the 20 and 50 yard lines on each side of the massive stadium. "I think I liked it better when we played at Bovard Field. You could see the players' faces."

"The school administrators figure that, with all this room, all we have to do is have a few championship teams to fill the stadium. At a dollar a seat, that's a lot of money for the athletic program. I've been told the coaches are recruiting some great high school football players to help bring in the crowds. Long Beach High School has a kid at quarterback named Morley Drury who might be the best high school player in the nation."

"Well, good luck to them. Next time we play here, I'll bring binoculars."

"The West Coast eliminations for the Olympic Team will also be here next May."

She grinned. "So the Coliseum officials have an alternate plan. All of Los Angeles will be here to watch handsome David defeat a bunch of big ugly Goliaths."

"David has to get much better with his rock and sling to make that happen."

The Trojan team came running out of the tunnel and onto the field interrupting any further conversation. The team was accompanied by a roar much louder than Bud or Dawn had previously experienced.

"There does seem to be a new tingle of excitement in this stadium," Dawn admitted.

USC's old nemesis, the California Bears, ran out onto the field accompanied by many boos and catcalls with only a few cheers.

Like the Washington game at Seattle and the beginning of the Stanford game at Palo Alto, the young USC line was unable to stop their opponents running game, and Cal went ahead 7 to 0. The teams exchanged possession several times with neither able to move the ball until Cal scored again just before the half to take a 13-to-0 lead into the locker room.

Bud took the steps two at a time and returned a few minutes later with two green Coke bottles and three hot dogs loaded down with mustard, relish, and chopped onions. "All this for 25 cents," he said with a grin. "Beats the prices at Stanford."

In the second half, USC finally held the Bears offense in check and scored a touchdown of their own, but it was too little and too late. California defeated the Trojan's once again, this time by a score of 13 to 7.

*   *   *

"Why does Cal beat us so often?" Dawn complained as Bud drove her Packard Twin-Six toward their engagement announcement party at her parents' house. "Do they have better coaches?"

"You're beginning to sound like a true Trojan fan. We hate to lose, and when we do, the easiest person to blame is the coach."

"Well, then, who is to blame?"

"They recruit some great athletes up north. I just hope that our track team can win at Berkley this year."

Dawn sat with her arms folded. Apparently she didn't totally let the coach off the hook. Then, a big smile lit up her face. She held up her left hand, called out "Whoo whoo," and waved it around for drivers and passengers of other cars to see her engagement ring. A few drivers honked their horns. Then she scooted over and put her head on his shoulder. "Forget football. Tonight we will officially tell everyone that we are going to get married."

He put one arm around her and steered with the other. "So, you're saying most of our friends and family already know we're engaged, but they won't officially know until tonight?"

"Men just don't understand these things."

"You're right about that."

Chapter 27

There were giants yet to conquer at the beginning of track season during Bud's sophomore year at the University of Southern California. The invincibility he had enjoyed in high school had been replaced with the challenge to exceed the shot put and discus marks being set by bigger and older men. How could he have conquered Olympic champion Pat McDonald in the 12 pound shot while still in high school, and then lost to him in the 16-pound shot in the New York AAU championship a year later? Gus Pope, Thomas Lieb, and even his friend, Swede Anderson, had all defeated him at least once during his freshman year. Up north, Stanford had a new weight man named Glenn "Tiny" Hartcranft who was putting the shot out an amazing 50 feet and flinging the discus over 151 feet. The San Francisco Athletic Club boasted about Morris Kirksey whose marks were almost equal to Hartcranft's.

Bud's Trojan friends, Leighton Dye, Otto Anderson, Yale Martz, and Swede Anderson, as well as his old high school buddy, Cliff Argue of Occidental College, were also struggling to combat the Olympic-year pressure. Newspapers nationwide, heaping accolades on Bud and predicting he would eventually triumph over all his competitors provided an added incentive for him to succeed. Some people claimed he was too young to have reached his peak and advised him to shoot for the 1928 or 1932 Olympics. Bud planned to be practicing dentistry before even the first of those two events had occurred. The 1924 Olympic tryouts were only a few months off and that's where his focus would remain.

*   *   *

Famous newspaper columnist, Maxwell Stiles, wrote, "Clay of the earth taken from the Baldwin Hills of Arcadia and laid down hard and firm in the most modern athletic plant in the country served the pounding feet of Southern California's greatest athletes in the Sixth Annual Amateur Athletic Union Relay Carnival. This meet, ended in a blaze of glory for the varsity and freshman teams in the magnificent new Los Angeles Coliseum."

Bud won both the shot put and discus in the relays but knew his distances would need to be better in future meets. Swede Anderson finished second behind Bud in the shot put with a toss of over 45 feet. The final scores were USC Varsity 33 points, USC Frosh 21 points, Pomona 14 points, Los Angeles Athletic Club 11 points, and high school champion, Huntington Beach, 9 points. Trojans teams were beginning to assert themselves as future collegiate and Olympic champions, and the Los Angeles Coliseum provided the site where it all would happen.

*   *   *

The reunion of Bud Houser and Cliff Argue at the USC-Occidental track meet was bittersweet. The two of them had confounded opponents with their athletic abilities while at Oxnard High School, winning championships in basketball and baseball as well as track. Now Cliff was alternating between competing in the high jump, broad jump, dashes, and hurtles. Being good enough to win some meets in any of those events was both a blessing and a curse. Bud, on the other hand, was struggling to find time for his dental classes, practicing for the weight events, and traveling to various locations for track meets.

Bud put the shot out to 46 feet 10 inches and flung the discus 141 feet, good enough for wins over his closest competitor, Swede Anderson, but not good enough to please himself. He noticed that, whatever distance he reached, Swede very often performed just well enough to take second place. "Are you holding back so you can surprise me in the Olympic Finals?" he asked.

Swede laughed and slapped Bud on the back. "I'm not clever enough to come up with an idea like that. I was wondering why, no matter how well I do, you always do just enough better to win."

They walked across the field in time to watch Cliff Argue edge out Yale Martz in the 100-yard dash, and then hold on to beat Yale in the 220 before the Trojan could quite close the gap separating the two men. During the second race, Bud noticed for the first time that Yale ran the second half of the race in almost the same time as the first. When the time was announced at just over twenty-two seconds, he felt certain Yale would be going to Paris to compete in the longer race. He felt no urgency to tell him. Yale was smart enough to figure that out for himself.

The final score was USC 81, Occidental 50. Bud had a moment of regret that he and Cliff Argue hadn't graduated from Oxnard High School the same year. He was sure, had that been the case, Cliff would also be a Trojan.

*   *   *

A few weeks later, USC easily beat Pomona 90 to 50 with Bud again finishing first, and Swede taking second in the shot and discus. Next week, the Trojans would travel up north to meet their old nemesis, the California Bears. Bud, along with every other man on the squad, couldn't wait to give Cal a good whipping on their home field.

*   *   *

Dawn jumped out of her car, raced up the walkway of the Sigma Chi house and burst through the door. When she was near the top of the stairs, she heard a voice call out, "You can't go up there!"

"Where is Bud?" she asked a startled frat member.

He pointed toward a closed door at the end of the hall, and said, "You're not supposed to be…"

"Yes, I know. Someone already told me."

Approaching the easy chair where Bud was sitting, she was startled at how pale he looked. "Honey, you look terrible."

"Ain't that a kick in the teeth," he squeaked.

"What did your doctor say?"

"He said I need to have my tonsils out."

"Let me drive you to the hospital. I've heard tonsillitis can develop into something more serious if you don't take care of it right away."

"I can't go this week. I have to be in Berkley for the track meet against Cal."

"Oh, please no. Don't tell me you plan to compete in the track meet in this condition."

"The doctor came here and examined me." He paused for a few seconds to rest his voice. "He said it should be okay for me to wait until Monday for surgery."

"Sure, he's probably a big Trojan fan and wants to beat California more than protect you." She sat down and put her hand over her face. "Isn't there anything that I can say to change your mind? If you go up there and then die of pneumonia or something, I'll never forgive you."

He laughed a soprano kind of sound, and then held his throat. "The doctor gave me some medicine to sooth my throat. I promise you can take me to the hospital the first thing Monday morning."

One of the older members of the fraternity came in and told Dawn she wasn't allowed to be there.

She held the third finger of her left hand up toward the man, and then kissed Bud on the forehead. "I'll call you on the phone, sweetheart."

"You were showing him your engagement ring, right?"

"Of course I was, sweetheart."

Chapter 28

March 22, 1924

Berkley Stadium in Strawberry Canyon was a sea of umbrellas. Rain arrived early in the morning at the University of California campus and it appeared it was going to stay around for a while. While waiting for their events to begin, Bud and Swede wandered around the muddy field finding the best vantage points to watch their team perform. This year USC had the talent to win, but many wondered if the jinx the Bears held over the Trojans had run its course. Bud's sore throat prevented him from cheering when his friend Leighton Dye won the 220 high hurdles four yards ahead of Cal's Jim Barber, but he let out a yell of dismay when the officials disqualified Leighton for knocking down three hurdles. He slipped a menthol lozenge into his mouth and promised himself not to repeat this mistake.

In spite of Leighton's disqualification and the wet sloppy track, it appeared the Trojans had too much talent for the Bears this year. Cal's Jim Barber ignored the muddy track, winning the 100 yard dash a half a step in front of Yale Martz in a surprising time of 9.9 seconds. After that, the Trojans ran off a string of victories. Elwood won the mile run. Hughes won the 440. White easily took the pole vault. Ross upset Cal's Goblick in the high jump, and Wilson won the broad jump. Bud suppressed any vocal display of excitement when his pal Otto Anderson made up a two yard disadvantage in the anchor leg of a record-breaking win in the relay, and then took second in the broad jump. After Yale Martz finished a close second to speedster Jim Barber in the

220, Bud and Swede walked over to the shot put ring feeling pretty good about the team's chances of finally whipping their old nemesis.

As soon as Bud picked up the 16 pound ball, he knew he should have listened to Dawn's advice. He went through his regular pre-throw routine, determined to summon up enough strength to make at least one good effort, but the ball landed far short of his usual distance. Swede came through with a throw of 44 feet 6 inches to lead the Bears' star weight man, Neufeldt, after the first round. With Swede's performance adding to all the other Trojan heroics, Bud felt like his trip up north was not only unwise but also unnecessary.

In spite of the mud under his feet, the soaking rain, and the feeling that someone had cut his throat, Bud somehow pushed the shot put a little over 40 feet to capture third place. Swede won the event with a personal best of 45 feet 11 inches, and Neufeldt took second place.

When Bud congratulated the big man, Swede was shocked at his high raspy voice.

"Why don't you go in the locker room? You should dry out and get into some warm clothes. It looks like we're going to win this one anyway."

Due to the pain in his throat, Bud attempted to communicate using as few words as possible. "Leighton disqualified already gives them three first places, and they're taking an awful lot of seconds and thirds."

Swede put his arm around Bud. "Don't talk anymore. I see what you mean. They have twice as many men here as we do. Neufeldt will probably win the Javelin, but maybe we can beat him in the discus."

Coach Cromwell joined the two weight men, "Why don't you hang 'em up for today, Bud. We're going to beat these guys easily at the Olympic tryouts. That's the one that that counts."

"I'm okay, Coach. One more event isn't going to hurt me."

Neufeldt was still feeling the sting of losing the shot put to the Trojans' second best weight man and was determined to not let it happen twice. Somehow Bud got off one good throw to take second place behind Neufeldt, but Francis of Cal took third place. Swede finished fifth.

*   *   *

No one was unhappier on the train ride back to Los Angeles than Leighton Dye. His disqualification in the 120 yard hurdles had given the California Bears nine unearned points and allowed them to win still one more victory over USC. Although the Trojans had won more events, Cal had won enough second and third places to squeeze out a 67-to-63 win over the stronger, but smaller, USC squad. Leighton sat with Otto, Swede and Bud hashing over their defeat.

Across the aisle from them, Yale Martz was too discouraged to respond to Leighton's shouldering the blame. He had taken second place to Jim Barber in both the dashes. Convinced he had run his best races, he was amazed that anyone could run a 9.9 second 100-yard-dash and 22.4 second 220 on such a sloppy track. The worst part was Barber was an underclassman who would probably get even better. This was Yale's senior year at USC, and his last chance to do something significant. He had been unable to beat Jim Barber of Cal or Cliff Argue of Occidental in either of the dashes. He could see his chances of going to Paris fading away. Bundled up with a warm coat and a blanket, the voices of Bud and his friends blurred together, and then faded out as sleep overtook the discouraged sprinter.

Chapter 29

When Bud's eyes popped open, the first face he saw was Dawn's. He looked at her for a moment, and then pursed his lips and turned his head.

"It hurts that bad?"

He made a slashing sign with his finger across his throat.

"Don't try to talk. Just nod or shake your head. Does it hurt worse now than it did before surgery?"

His pained expression told her more than the nodding of his head.

"The doctor said you will be weaker for a while, but that you shouldn't worry about that."

He raised his eyebrows.

"Please promise me you won't compete in any track meets until you're better."

He took his index finger and made an "X" on his heart.

"Why don't I believe you?"

He shrugged.

"Is there anything you want me to get for you while I'm here?"

"Chocolate ice cream." he squeaked.

"Really? You want me to bring you some ice cream?"

He grinned and shook his head.

"I see that they didn't remove your sense of humor. I think this whole thing has been harder on me than you."

He nodded in agreement.

Your sister and my mother are in the waiting room, so I don't want to take up too much of their time, but before I go, I have some things to show you." She picked up a newspaper. "Every sports columnist in town has a write-up about your operation. Harry Hayward even wrote about you on page one of the Los Angeles Times. She held up the paper with headlines that read, "HOUSER UNDER KNIFE TODAY." Everyone is speculating about whether you will be at full strength in time for the AAU meet at the Coliseum. Sid Ziff thinks you will, and Maxwell Stiles isn't so sure. All Robert Ray can talk about is how brave you were to compete up at Berkley."

Bud winced.

"Honey, I don't care how long it takes you to get well. I'm just glad your surgery is over. I know a tonsillectomy isn't supposed to be very dangerous, but, until the doctor came out and said you were okay, I was scared to death."

He squeezed her hand.

"I came here to comfort you, and now you're consoling me."

"I would feel worse if it was you lying here," he whispered. Glancing at the stack of newspapers she'd brought into his hospital room, he asked. "Why are so many people rooting for me to win? Is it because I was an orphan?"

"You shouldn't be talking so much. You could end up becoming a soprano. I'm going leave so you can rest. I'll tell my mother and your sister not to stay too long."

He took hold of her wrist.

"You want me to tell you why you're famous?" She put her chin on her hand and pretended she was solving a difficult equation. "It's probably a combination of things, but the main reason, as you already know, is because you're so darn good-looking. And being engaged to a gorgeous USC coed like me helps a lot, too. Any other questions, genius?"

He laughed, winced in pain, and then gently ran his fingers across his sore throat.

She leaned over and kissed him. "Don't talk anymore, honey."

Chapter 30

Breakfast in the Sigma Chi house dining hall was served from seven to eight and was accompanied by copies of the LA Times, LA Examiner, and a few out-of-town newspapers. Boys who were quickly becoming men took an interest in international, national, and local news. This morning a piano concerto played by pianist, Violet Pearch, could be heard from the radio in the living room, while plates of scrambled eggs and bacon, hotcakes, and pitchers of coffee were passed down the long tables. A few commerce majors huddled in one corner discussing their small, but carefully managed, stock portfolios, and discussing whether the stock exchange could sustain its lofty 85 point level. On the other side of the room, some of the literary-minded students disputed the comparative merits of F. Scott Fitzgerald, Sinclair Lewis, and William Faulkner. By far, the largest numbers of Sigma Chi members were pouring through the sports pages.

Claire Kennedy, who nicely filled the role of surrogate mother as well as cook for her brood, had prepared a special breakfast of oatmeal with brown sugar, bananas, and milk for her ailing one. Bud was preparing to pile some bacon and hotcakes onto his plate, when one of Claire's long, dusky hands reached down and stopped him. With the other hand, she placed the oatmeal in front of him.

"Please Claire," Bud whispered, "I need to get my strength back."

She shook her head. "This will be better for you, Mister Houser. If you don't get enough to eat, I'll fix some poached eggs and milk toast for you."

No matter how many fraternity members tried, they could not persuade their favorite cook to address them by their first names, however, no one doubted that in the kitchen and dining room, she was and always would be the boss. When alumni visited, they often claimed that eating another meal cooked by Claire was the real reason they were there.

Bud held the Herald Examiner sports page in front of him while gingerly testing mildly-hot coffee passing through his throat.

"You have to see this one," Ben Gerpheide said as he laid a Long Beach Press Telegram across Bud's Examiner.

Bud looked at an artist's conception of himself, Tiny Hartcranft, and New York cop, Pat McDonald, looking toward the ocean as two Finnish champion weight men looked frightened. The bubble caption depicting what the Finns were saying read, "I see your Finnish," and underneath it read, "Parmola and Nicklender of Finland are worried sick about Bud, Tiny and Pat."

Bud grinned and tossed the paper back to Ben. "If only that were true."

"If I were them, I'd be worried."

"How is the football team shaping up for next year?"

"What did you say?" Ben asked.

Bud pointed to his throat and repeated, "Football team…next year?"

"Oh. Our new coach, Howard Jones, is bringing in some great recruits, and he's scheduling some tougher intersectional teams for us to play. We plan to start filling up the coliseum this next year."

"Wow! That's a lot of seats to fill."

"You bet it is, especially when we had 10,800 the first time we played there last fall. How many people are you expecting for the AAU meet next Saturday?"

"We won't fill up the coliseum, but there should be between 30,000 and 40,000."

"Are you going to be at full strength by then?"

Bud nodded.

As if she was on cue, Claire set a plate of three poached eggs lying atop buttered milk toast in between the newspapers. "You don't have to eat all of this," she said.

Ben waited until Claire disappeared back into the kitchen before wrinkling his nose and asking, "Are you really going to eat that stuff?"

"When you grow up on a farm, you learn to appreciate whatever food is available," Bud said as he plunged his fork into a soft egg yolk.

Chapter 31

Jack Dempsey threw a series of left jabs that landed flush on his opponent's face and then, when the man's hands were raised to protect his jaw, he stepped in and delivered a lethal uppercut to the other fighter's midsection. He started a right cross toward the left side of the challenger's head. Mercifully, the Manassa Mauler pulled the punch and allowed his adversary to crumple to the floor. The referee jumped between the two men and stopped the fight. Dempsey was actually a kind man. Hurting or embarrassing his opponents was not his style, but, as many challengers had learned, when you were throwing punches at the champion, you better be prepared to take some punishment.

Bud had always thought the world's heavyweight champion was a bigger man and was surprised to find that Dempsey was about his size. The three opponents he had knocked out in the first round of this set of exhibition matches had all been inches taller and much heavier than the champ.

"He's a lot like you," Otto Anderson remarked as members of the Trojan track team left the area around the boxing ring and headed toward the other side of the field toward Coach Cromwell.

"If he's like me, why did those kids ask for your autograph this morning?"

Otto chuckled. "Okay, apparently I'm a Jack Dempsey look-alike. What I meant was he's an average size guy whipping men who are much bigger than him. That's what you've been doing ever since you were in high school."

Bud looked toward the coliseum seats closest to the shot put and discus rings. Dawn said she would wear a white hat with a red ribbon on it, but one person in such a sea of faces was impossible for him to locate.

"Have you guys ever seen anything like this?" Swede asked.

"There seems to be almost as many people on the field as in the stands," Yale Martz said.

"I read where there would be over 400 athletes competing today," Bud said.

"With about 600 coaches, referees, and VIPs mingling in," Swede added.

"I've told you a million times not to exaggerate," Yale scolded.

Coach Dean Cromwell waved members of his team over to a spot on the grass nearest the closed end of the coliseum. When all had gathered, he said. "Our goal today is to qualify as many members of our team as possible for the semifinals in Cambridge. With that in mind, I'm making a few changes that will have some of you competing in events different than what you've been used to. I've been told our former teammate, Charlie Paddock, is only going to run the 200 meters. He'll win it easily and qualify for the semis back East. Cliff Argue from Oxy is the man to beat in the hundred. I have you, Smith and you Lloyd, scheduled for that race."

Yale Martz looked at his friends in disbelief. Sure, he'd been finishing second and third behind Argue and a few other sprinters, but the races were close. He couldn't believe that the coach wasn't going to give him one more chance.

The coach continued, "Martz, I want you to run the 400 meter, and Otto Anderson you'll be competing in the broad jump. Houser, of course you and Swede will be competing in the shot and discus, but I want you, Bud, to also try to win us a medal in the hammer throw. Okay, men; let's show these other schools that we own this place. From now on the Los Angeles Coliseum is our home field, and we don't want anyone to forget it."

Bud put his arm around his downcast friend. "Yale, I believe the coach knows what he's doing. You're going to win the 400 meter."

"I've never run a race that long. I don't know how to pace myself."

"And Otto has only occasionally competed in the broad jump, but Cromwell must figure he's a good enough athlete to make the adjustment. One thing I've noticed is, after a race, you aren't as tired as the guys you run against. Don't try to pace yourself. Give it all you've got the whole way around the track. I'm betting you're going to blow those other guys away."

Excitement continued to build among the near 40,000 people attending the Southern California Olympic tryouts. The Trojan Band marched out onto the field and played the national anthem, and then the competition was underway.

The loudest cheers of the day were when Bud pushed the shot put out three-and-one-half inches short of 50 feet, and then flung the discus 142 feet 5 inches. Swede Anderson finished second in both events. Bud was especially happy with his showing because he knew he wasn't yet at full strength. He did, however have to factor in that Hartcranft of Stanford and Lieb of California at Berkeley, each for individual reasons, had been unable to compete. Both of them, along with many other top weight men, would be at Cambridge and Boston. As almost an afterthought, Bud strolled over to the hammer throw and finished third.

Because of Coach Cromwell's assignment of different events to Otto Anderson and Yale Martz, members of the Trojan team who weren't competing in other events at that time gathered to watch their two teammates perform.

Yale started like he was running the 100 meters making Bud apprehensive that he'd given his friend poor advice. He heard a man's voice saying, "He'll never keep up that pace." Rounding the last turn, Yale was so far out in front of the other runners, the only question was, would he fade at the end?

After the race, Yale's face was deep-red as he leaned over with his hands on his knees gasping for breath. Bud and other Trojans mobbed him, slapping him on the back and yelling their congratulations. Over the coliseum loudspeaker, they heard, "Ladies and Gentleman, Yale Martz of USC has won the 400 meters in the record-breaking time of 49.4 seconds. It seems the 400 meters has now become another sprint."

Otto Anderson finished a close second behind Trojan freshman, Kaer, with surprising a jump of 24 feet 4 1/2 inches. This easily qualified him for a trip back east.

Bud's thin, light-haired friend, the always-improving Leighton Dye, tied Daggs of the LA Athletic Club in the 120 yard low hurdles to give the victorious USC team an overpowering 76 points with the USC Frosh adding another 33 points. The Trojan Varsity and Frosh scored more points than all of their opponents put together.

*   *   *

The huge house at 4104 West Pico was lit up like a Christmas tree. Dr. and Cora Smith were entertaining all 16 members of the Trojan track team who had qualified to go back East to Cambridge for the Olympic semifinals, as well as a few others who had not made the cut. To make the evening more interesting, Dawn had invited a group of her DeeGee fraternity sisters. Mama Smith had hired two young ladies to pass out soft drinks and refreshments to assure that she would have plenty of time to spend with her guests. The celebrity guests were Dr. Smith's friend, Jack Dempsey, and his wife, Estelle Taylor.

Bud sipped a cold drink while visiting with Otto Anderson and his new bride, Hazel Bobbitt Anderson. As he watched Dawn going around the room making sure all the guests were enjoying themselves and introducing unescorted DeeGees to unattached athletes, he realized for the first time how much his high-spirited fiancée' took after her father. He looked across the room at Dr. Smith's broad grin as he posed for a picture with one arm around Jack Dempsey and the other one around Coach Dean Cromwell. His mind drifted again to the anguish he had felt when his father had died, and the way Martha's husband, Walter Conklin, had become a surrogate father to him. Now he was anticipating the growth of his already warm relationship with his future father-in-law.

Dawn's father was everything Bud wanted to be. Dr. Smith had achieved much more than just financial success. He generously gave to the Pico Avenue Christian Church, as well as being a key supporter of the university. Bud was constantly amazed at how many famous people he counted as his friends. He was also a doting father and a faithful husband. Maybe his cry had been heard when his father had died, and he had decided that God didn't like him. Between Walter Conklin and Dr. Smith, Bud would have not one, but two father figures.

Dr. Smith spotted Bud and made his way over to introduce Dempsey and his wife to his future son-in law.

When the champ met the Andersons, he said to Otto, "I feel like I'm looking into a mirror."

"Don't flatter yourself, honey," Estelle teased. "This young man is much better looking than you."

"Well, I think I can fix that," Jack said, doubling his fist and pretending to throw a punch at Otto. Jack turned to Bud, "How does a guy your size beat all those monsters in the shot and discus?"

"How does a guy your size whip all those brutes that are trying to take away your title?" Dr. Smith shot back.

"Very good point," Dempsey conceded.

Chapter 31

The pressure of trying out for the Olympic Games and its accompanying cruise from New York to Paris had not diminished the appetites of the group of Southern California's athletes having breakfast in the Lennox Hotel dining room in Cambridge. Bud's high school Buddy, Cliff Argue, now competing for Occidental College, had joined the Trojan contingent who was running the harried waitress back and forth from the kitchen to their tables bringing more hotcakes, bacon, and orange juice. The amount of food being consumed this morning was partly because of the youth and marvelous health of some of the country's foremost track-and-field stars, but also because, no matter how much they ate, all they had to do was write down their room numbers and sign the check.

Sitting across the table from Cliff Argue, Yale Martz recalled recent articles in Los Angeles newspapers that had listed neither he nor the speedster from Occidental among those predicted to win at Cambridge Stadium during the next couple of days or at the finals at Harvard Stadium in Boston in the coming week. Too many other dash men had times that excelled their best performances.

Bud appeared to be the only one who didn't believe he would be on the Olympic team by popular demand, even if his distances were surpassed by some bigger and older men. His friends had a clearer perception of the benefits he'd gained by catching the imagination of the American public while he was still in high school. The remainder of the diners, Swede Anderson, Otto Anderson, and Leighton Dye also had excellent chances to qualify for the Paris trip.

Swede heaped four more hotcakes on his plate and told Bud, "I better stop here. This will make twelve I've eaten."

"Actually that makes 16, but whose counting?" Bud said. "You do realize we're going up against the best weight-men in the country today."

Swede washed down a bite of food with his coffee. "I perform better with a full stomach. Which guy are you the most concerned about?"

"Let's see, other than you, I guess it would be Hills of Princeton...no, maybe Hartcranft of Stanford...no, I think I'm more worried about Lieb or Ashton from the Illinois Athletic Club...actually that New York cop. What's his name?"

"As if you didn't know the guy who put you on the map."

"That's right, Pat McDonald. I'm definitely most concerned about McDonald...no, I think...."

"Okay, I get the point. Do you feel you're back to full strength?"

Bud nodded.

Swede looked skeptical. "It looks to me like you're still down about 10 pounds."

"You don't have to be big to throw those little balls and plates out onto the grass."

"I believe I've discovered your secret. No one ever told you that you're built more like a sprinter than a weight man. You're not nearly big enough to be competing in the shot put and discus."

"You're kidding me! Do you think it's too late to change my event?"

Otto Anderson walked behind his two laughing team members. "You guys whistling past the graveyard?"

"Something like that," Swede answered. "I guess we better head out, Bud. We can't win any medals if we're not there."

"I'm more worried about the other guys who will be showing up," Cliff Argue said as he scooped up Bud and Swede's check on his way by.

"Hey, our friend from across town is buying our breakfast," Swede roared.

"It's the least I can do," Cliff said as he scribbled his signature across the bottom of each check. "Let's catch the bus."

*　　　*　　　*

Cambridge, New Jersey provided a perfect day for the second to last elimination for the 1924 Olympics. Any athlete with a poor performance would have to provide an excuse other than the weather. Swede put the shot 46 feet 3 inches on his first toss giving him the lead after the first round. When Bud discovered how heavy the 16 pound ball felt balanced on his hand, he knew he still wasn't at full strength. The cheering crowd propelled him to a toss of an even 49 feet on his second try, but he knew from the weakness in his knees that that effort would have to hold up for him to win. He was still in the lead going into the final throw but was only able to toss the shot put 44 feet 11 inches.

The officials marked Stanford University star, Glenn Hartcranft's, last throw at 49 feet 5 ¾ inches putting him in first place and Bud in second place with only Hills of Princeton with one attempt remaining. Spectators and athletes were surprised when the official placed Hills' flag at exactly the same distance as Hartcranft's. It was a safe bet that both men would be on the ship to Paris, but still a tie in an Olympic tryout was sure to cause some dispute. Another official didn't calm the state of affairs when he leaned down with his nose a few feet from the flags and declared that Hartcranft had won by one-eighth of an inch.

"No official can be that accurate," Swede said. "Even if the flags are an eighth of an inch apart, how can anyone place one of them that accurately?"

"I would have to agree. Anyway, the important thing is you finished fourth, and I finished third."

"And you're still not at full strength."

"Did I say I wasn't at full strength?"

Swede put his arm around Bud as they walked toward where their teammates were competing. "If we can do as well in Boston, we both should be on the ship to Paris."

After watching Leighton Dye take a second and Otto Anderson a third in the hurdles, they all rooted Cliff Argue on to a surprising third-place finish in the broad jump and a fourth in the relay. Cliff Martz was not so fortunate. The smallest member of their group, at 150 pounds, sprained an ankle, missed placing in the 400-meter dash, and suffered the heartbreak of not qualifying for the finals in Boston.

Later that day, Bud regained enough strength to fling the discus 154 feet 11 inches. When Hills' final toss landed right on Bud's marker, the officials wisely ruled it a tie for second behind Hartcranft's amazing throw of 158 feet 8 inches.

During dinner that night, conversation centered on past victories and amusing anecdotes. Swede embellished the episode involving the hiking trip to Canada, the girl he'd met on the Niagara Falls cruise, and subsequent poor showing of the reckless Los Angeles Athletic Club representatives. This narration caused a few athletes to almost choke on their food. No mention was made of Cliff Martz's bad luck. The sad, but unspoken fact was that the competition today had been the last track meet this senior at USC would be able to enjoy with his friends.

*　　*　　*

The crowd was bigger and the pressure even greater as some of the best athletes in the world gathered in Boston in the final elimination for the 1924 Olympics. After a lackluster performance on the first day of the Olympic finals in Boston, Bud and his friends entered the second of the two day competition still needing some medals to guarantee their trip to the Olympics in Paris.

Bud had made the best showing of the day when he tied Glenn Hartcranft for fourth in the discus with a toss of 144 feet 7 inches. This provided neither the USC nor the Stanford athlete any guarantee about their chances of qualifying for the Olympics. Thomas Lieb had taken first place when he hurled the saucer 153 feet 6 inches while his teammate at the Illinois Athletic Club, Gus Pope, was close behind at 150 feet 10 inches.

Some fifth and sixth-place showings by the other Pacific Coast men counted toward making the team, but left them anxious about being edged out by only a few points. The disappointment experienced by Yale Martz at Cambridge weighed on their minds.

Otto and Cliff relieved some pressure on this last day of the tryouts, when they reeled off third-place finishes, Cliff in the 200-meter dash and Otto in the broad jump. Winners of first, second and even fourth and fifth places in these events were athletes considered among the best in the world.

Bud picked up the 16-pound ball and was relieved that it felt lighter than just a few days before at Cambridge. He had read an article in the Los Angeles Times last week that predicted that Hartcranft would win the shot put, Bud would finish second, and Swede Anderson would take fourth. Eastern newspapers he'd read since then had predictably been less generous with their predictions about the westerners' performance.

As soon as the shot left Bud's hand, he knew it was a good throw. When the official marked it at 49 feet 11 inches, he felt sure his first throw would be tough to beat, even by the talented men he was competing against.

Bud observed how pressure appeared to be bothering some of the athletes and wondered how much greater it would be at Paris. He was thankful that his early training made him stronger and more determined when his back was against the wall. When the last man had finished, Bud's toss had stood up against all challenges, guaranteeing him a spot on the Olympic team with this unexpected first place finish. In an even bigger surprise, Swede Anderson beat Hartcranft for second place, not only guaranteeing him a trip to Paris, but making him one of the favorites for a medal at Paris.

Out of courtesy for their disappointed competitors, Bud and Swede withheld any outward show of emotion until they reached the locker room. Once there, they began dancing and yelling loud enough to attract onlookers who thought a fight had broken out.

Chapter 32

Dawn was still grinning when she wheeled her Packard Twin-Six into the driveway of her home on Pico Boulevard. If anyone in her art classes hadn't seen the headline and her picture in the Herald Examiner, they had certainly heard about it from those who had.

When she'd sat down at the breakfast table this morning, her father had turned the paper around for her to see – "BUD HOUSER TO WED USC COED IN PARIS."

Her eyes had widened, her jaw dropped open, and she shook her head. "I don't know a thing about this."

Dr. Smith's normal jovial smile had been replaced by a worried frown. "Do you think Bud was planning to surprise us?"

She looked at her picture and wondered where the newspaper had obtained it, and then read down the page, "TRACK STAR ALSO LUCKY WITH CUPID. Reliable sources have informed the Herald Examiner about Bud Houser's plan to wed Dawn Evelyn Smith, daughter of Dr. and Mrs. C.C. Smith of Los Angeles. The romantic couple will be traveling to the Olympic Games with the United States Olympic team aboard the S.S America and plan to recite their vows while in Paris… " She stopped reading and took a quick breath.

"Dawn, you know how disappointed your mother will be if her only daughter said her wedding vows without her there."

"I thought you and mom planned go to Paris for the games."

Instead of answering Dr. Smith had put his hand on his daughter's cheek and smiled. "I know you will do what's right."

Dawn jumped out of the car and raced up the front steps two at a time. As soon as she walked into the sitting room, she heard her mother call from the kitchen.

"You're home early, Dad," she said while pulling a chair up to the kitchen table.

Again her father's face looked somber. "We have something important we need to talk to you about, honey."

She held up her hands toward her patents. "Before you start, I want you both to know that I will not be married anyplace but in the Pico Avenue Christian Church, and all my family and friends will be there."

She waited to see their look of relief, but none came.

"I was already sure of that," her mother said with a flickering of a smile. "We need to talk to you about something else."

"This sounds serious."

Finally her father's face broke into a familiar grin. "It's nothing for you to worry about, especially now with this exciting trip coming up. Your mother and I are going to visit family in Jeffersonville and will not be able to come to Paris."

"Why? We can see our relatives in Indiana any time."

"Your father is going into Clark Memorial Hospital for some tests."

A tear quickly formed on Dawn's cheek. "What's the matter, Dad?"

"I'm just having some routine tests. I've had a few chest pains recently, and I know and trust all the doctors back home. I need to be in top shape to keep up with those grandchildren when they begin to arrive."

"Couldn't the tests wait until we get back?"

"Until we know more about your father's condition, we feel it's better not to be out in the middle of the Atlantic Ocean."

"I want you and Bud to join your mother and me on your way home. It's a little early for the fall leaves, but you can show Bud the Ohio River, Camp Joe, and the falls."

"You're sure they are just routine tests?"

"Hey, your father is a tough old guy. You just have a great time in Europe."

Chapter 33

July 1924

The presence of the entire United States Olympic team aboard one ship bound for Paris rivaled the excitement team members felt for the upcoming games. Both male and female tennis players aboard the S.S. America fraternized with men and women on the swimming team. Bulky wrestlers and tough-looking boxers were reminded of their vincibility by men from the free-rifle and rapid-fire pistol teams. The pressure of competition would again be primary once the games began, but for now, team members basked in the glory of winning the honor of representing their country in this the most important athletic competition of their lives. Bud and Dawn looked forward to being spectators at the games for almost two weeks before competition in the weight events began.

Dawn's picture in newspapers nationwide, speculating about where and when the couple would wed, made her one of the most recognizable of the ship's passengers. Her athleticism had given her a toned body almost equal to swimmer, Gertrude Ederle, and tennis player, Helen Wills.

Standing on the deck in overcoats and hats and looking across a seemingly endless sea, Dawn wondered when Bud would bring up the subject of the news-report in the Los Angeles Herald Examiner and all the conjecture that had followed. As romantic as a wedding in Paris and a honeymoon in Europe sounded, she could not ignore all the hopes and plans her mother had for the marriage of her only daughter. Any surprise Bud was planning would somehow have to be stopped, but how should she approach the subject without hurting his feelings? She had thrown numerous hints his way, but so far none had provoked a response.

Bud said, "Can you imagine anything more exciting than this?"

"Actually I can," Dawn said. "I wish I was on the team."

"No kidding? What can you do?"

"I can throw a runner out at second, or I can sink fifteen-out-of-twenty free throws."

"I haven't seen either of those events listed, but I did hear that women will be competing in track events in 1928. How fast are you?"

"Not fast enough. I didn't feel like I was missing out on anything until I saw how many women are on the Olympic team."

"If you didn't know about the women, maybe I was wrong thinking you came on the trip just to keep an eye on me."

"Not completely. I just thought I only had to worry about the French girls."

"How about me worrying? I've seen some of the guys on the swimming team looking at Dr. Smith's famous daughter."

She thought about asking his opinion about the cause for her fame, and then decided to wait for a more private setting. "I haven't noticed."

"Anyone in particular you haven't noticed?"

"Now that you mention it, I think the ones I haven't noticed most would be Johnny Weissmuller and that tall dark Hawaiian, Duke Kahanamoku."

"Ouch! Those are two good-looking guys."

Swede and Otto heard Bud's last comment as they joined the pair.

"See, I told you they were talking about us," Swede said.

In his wool overcoat and straw hat, the big Swede looked even more like a giant than usual. Noticing the disparity between Swede's size and his own small companion, Bud decided this moment should be recorded.

Taking his box camera from its shoulder strap, he said, "Dawn, you and Swede stand up against the rail. Swede, you can put your arm around her, but don't squeeze."

Next, Swede took a picture of Bud, Dawn, and Otto, and then he asked, "Has anyone seen the gymnasts working out? Frank Kritz is putting on quite a show on the vault."

"Sounds good to me," Dawn said.

"What else is going on?" Bud asked.

"The women's swim team is doing some stretching and warm-up exercises on the lower deck." Swede glanced at Dawn, and then added, "If you find that sort of thing interesting."

One look at Dawn's expressionless face, and Bud said, "Let's go watch the gymnasts."

*   *   *

On the first evening aboard ship, Bud had escorted Dawn and his sister, Martha, into the ship's dining room, helped each into their chair, and then sat between them. This evening, as they neared the end of their journey across the Atlantic Ocean, nothing had changed. Rounding out their table of eight were Otto Anderson, Leighton Dye, Cliff Argue, Glenn Hartcranft, and Swede Anderson. The fact that they were three of the top weight men in the world, who would soon be competing for the biggest prize of their lives, did not detract from the spirit of friendship and camaraderie enjoyed by Bud, Swede, and Glenn. Each of them knew they would be close friends long after the final ceremonies had ended.

Bud looked over his combination menu and evening program. Only the food offered and the selection of dance music changed from one night to the next. On the back of the cover, under the *"Musical Programme,"* were the words "We are indebted to Miss Dawn Evelyn Smith for the following suggestions – Hors d' oeuvre - Puree Gibier – Boiled Red Snapper – Ox Tongue Polonaise – Roast Chicken with Dressing – Compote of Pineapple – Cake with Ice Cream – Demi Tasse." Looking to the right side of his open menu, he looked down over at least three alternate choices for each course. "I think I'll take your suggestions for everything except I'll have the prime ribs of beef instead of chicken."

"Oh gee," Dawn said as she looked at her menu.

"Is something the matter?" Martha asked.

"Yeah, I suggested chicken to Commander Rind, and now the leg of lamb with mint sauce sounds much better. Do you think anyone will notice if I change?"

After dinner, Bud and Dawn danced the Fox Trot to Silver's "Yes, We have no Bananas," waltzed to Faust's, "From the Mountain's Summit," followed in rapid succession by three other dance numbers played by the ship's orchestra.

Seeing his partner showed no signs of slowing down, Bud finally begged off. "Honey, you're wearing me out. Mind if we sit out this next dance?"

No, of course not."

As soon as the couple was back at their table, the orchestra began playing "Angoisse d' Amour," the romantic ballad by Benatzky. Three young men jumped to their feet and raced across the room toward Dawn. Charlie Paddock made use of his sprinter ability to reach Dawn just ahead of tennis player, Vincent Richards, and platform diver, Albert White.

"Do you mind if I dance with your fiancée?" Charlie asked.

Bud forced a smile and nodded his head.

Watching Dawn in Charlie's arms, he was glad the former Trojan was not among the men she had mentioned "not noticing."

"Helen Wills is looking at you," Leighton Dye said. I think she wants you to ask her to dance."

"After I told Dawn she'd wore me out? I think I'd better take a rain check."

"I always knew you were the smart one in our group," Swede offered.

"That might not help," Leighton said. "Here she comes."

"I guess she doesn't win all those tennis championships by being shy," Martha concluded.

"Hi, Bud, I'm Helen. Would you like to dance?"

* * *

A half moon provided more than enough moonlight shining across the black rippling water to provide a romantic setting for more than a few new romances. The ratio of six or eight men for every woman brought out the competitive nature of male members of the Olympic team, and the female Olympians were making the most of it, taking their pick of male escorts. Couples standing along the starboard deck had put as much distance between one another as space allowed, but not enough distance to prevent Dawn from noticing that Glenn Hartcranft had somehow become a close friend of Sybil Bauer of the women's swim team. "Glenn and Sybil seem to be getting along quite well," she observed.

"They have a lot in common," he remarked and immediately wondered how he would get out of that slip of the tongue.

"You mean because they're both championship athletes?"

"Oh, that too, I guess. I was thinking because they both came from Northern California."

"Glenn grew up just a few miles from the USC campus."

"I meant Southern California."

She pushed her shoulder against him and leaned toward the ship's rail. She had waited until this last night aboard ship for Bud to mention something about the continuing flood of newspaper articles predicting a Paris wedding for them. Apparently he did not intend to share what he had done or said to provoke so much speculation. Obviously, the longer she waited, the more difficult her announcement would be. Taking hold of the lapels of his overcoat and looking up at him, she began, "Honey, I know how much you love me, and what you have planned is such a wonderful idea, but I promised my mother we wouldn't get married until we are back home."

He took her face in his hands and smiled down at her. "That is exactly what will happen. That's why I was so surprised when I saw the news release you gave to the Los Angeles Herald."

"I didn't…you're surprised…I don't understand. I thought you had told someone we were going to be married in Paris, and the word got out."

"I was still in Cambridge when I saw it in the New York Times. If you didn't give them the story, where did they get your picture?"

"I don't know about that first one, but the recent ones say "International Newsreel Photo." I have no idea when they were taken. If it wasn't me and it wasn't you, who gave the story to the Herald?"

"Maybe someone who thought the Olympic committee must have a good reason to let you and my sister travel on the same ship with the team. You know, there aren't many people who could have pulled that off."

"My dad helped."

"Sure he did, and the same young lady who made him sign a note to buy her a Packard Twin-Six just for behaving herself in high school convinced him of what a good idea it was."

She pulled his face down to hers and grinned, "I'm so relieved you weren't planning to surprise me."

"I feel pretty good about…" The rest of his sentence was cut off by her mouth pressed hard against his.

When they came up for air, he added, "Just because we're not getting married doesn't mean we can't have fun."

"I brought your sister along to make sure we don't have too much fun."

"You know me better than that."

Chapter 34

Martha washed down another bite of her bonbon with a sip of hot tea. "I feel decadent," she said and then picked up one more bonbon.

Dawn sipped her tea, and looked from the balcony of the Napoleon Hotel across the narrow street to the sidewalk cafés and small shops along the tree lined walkway leading to the Arc de Triomphe. "We might have to ask the Lord's forgiveness, but after we visit the Fountainebleau Palace and Notre Dame Cathedral, we're going to visit another one those delightful sidewalk cafes. I intend to eat every pastry in sight. Maybe, even have a glass of wine if you promise not to tell my parents."

"'A little wine for thy stomach's sake.' Did you say Bud won't be joining us?"

"His excuse was his coach wants the entire field team to stay in the Olympic Village and work on their distances."

"Do you think that's just an excuse?"

"I'm sure there is some truth in it, but you saw how his rear end was dragging yesterday during the last hour at the Louvre."

Martha laughed at her future sister-in-law's colorful language. "It's always amazed me how even the strongest men can't keep up with an ordinary woman when we're sightseeing or shopping."

Dawn clinked her teacup against Martha's. "Here's to two ladies who will never be ordinary."

*   *   *

Bud worked his right arm and shoulder in a circular motion, looked at the 60,000 empty seats in Stade Olymique de Colombes, and imagined how crowded and noisy they would be 10 days from now. He had pushed the shot put out nearly 50 feet in practice this morning, and Swede Anderson, Glenn Hartcranft, and Thomas Lieb all had similar distances. Bud had decided that in the end the winner would be the one who responded best to pressure. If the two giants from Finland, Vilho Niittymaa and Eero Lehtonen, who were practicing less than a hundred feet away, had distances as long as their grunts were loud, the United States team wouldn't stand a chance anyway. The Finn's had swept the weight events in the 1920 Olympics.

Yesterday, while Bud had been sightseeing with his sister and fiancée, his friends had taken the bus to the new Olympic pool in Tourelles, near the heart of the city, and watched some of the preliminary races of the swim teams from around the world.

"Are you going to join Dawn and Martha again today?" Swede asked.

"I plan to hang around with you guys. My guess is you're going back to Tourelles."

"You got that right. The men's 100, 200, and 400 meter preliminaries have been more fun to watch than any of us expected, and because of Glenn we're all going to root for Sybil Bauer in the 100 meter back stroke."

"It's hard to imagine that watching people swim could be that interesting."

"Wait until you get there."

*   *   *

Bud watched Johnny Weissmuller beat Samuel Kahanamoku in the fourth race of the preliminaries of the 100 meters and still wondered why his teammates had become so fixated with watching people swim. A couple races later he found out. With only 50 meters left in the 400 meter, Duke

146

Kahanamoku began closing the distance between him and leaders Arne Borg of Sweden and Andrew "Boy" Charlton of Australia. When "The Duke" pulled ahead with only six meters left in the race, he was yelling as loud as the other American athletes and spectators. The competition between countries was what made the difference.

The handsome Hawaiian shook the water off his long, black hair and grinned as he was being congratulated by his brother Samuel Kahanamoku and other teammates, Johnny Weissmuller and Robert Skelton.

"Was it just my imagination, or did Borg and Charlton ease up at the end of that race?" Bud asked.

"First, second, and third, all qualify for the finals," Glenn said. "Borg and Charlton didn't need to swim their best times."

"So there is some strategy to swim meets. Are Borg and Charlton favored to win the finals of the 400?"

"They are," Leighton Dye said, "But Johnny Weissmuller could pull an upset."

"So where does that leave Duke Kahanamoku?"

"Hopefully winning or taking second in the 100 meters," Leighton said.

"Wow. I could write a book on what I don't know about swim meets."

*   *   *

Feeding over 3000 athletes in the first-ever Olympic Village was not a task for the faint hearted. Retiring president of the IOC, Baron Pierre de Coubertine, was determined to erase any memories of what was still considered an ignominious debacle by his native country in the 1900 Olympics. This year, in spite of a disastrous flood the previous spring and some harsh financial difficulties, the city and country were proving more than up to the task. International rivalry at the Wimbledon and French Opens in tennis, the French and British Opens in golf, and cycling events throughout Europe had caught the imagination of sport fans around the world. As a result, competition between countries had become intense. This allowed sports writers to promote the 1924 Olympics as the greatest sporting event of all time.

Tonight, Southern California athletes gathered at the USA section of the great hall and consumed enormous quantities of food especially prepared with their health and vigor in mind. After dinner, Bud waited in line for one of the public telephones. Dawn answered on the third ring.

"Hi, sweetie, did you see the rest of Paris today?"

"It would take a year to see all of Paris."

"That will give us a reason to come back. Honey, you have to come with me to watch the men's finals in the swimming competition tomorrow. You can't believe how exciting they are."

"I'm sure I can arrange that. Who is this calling?"

"That's very funny. Seriously, I'm surprised that something I thought would be dull could be this interesting. Are you sure I'm not interrupting any of your plans?"

"No. Martha and I were just talking about taking a break from all of the walking and standing. Tell me what you will be wearing so I can find you."

Bud laughed. "That could get complicated. I'll be wearing the same red-white-and-blue shirt, jacket, and pants as all of the other American athletes. Why don't I meet you at the gate? You know how to get to Tourelles?"

"We'll find it."

Chapter 35

Even though they had never watched a swim meet before, Dawn and Martha were bubbling with excitement from the opening race, cheering loudly as Johnny Weissmuller barely edged out Arne Borg of Sweden and Andrew "Boy" Miller of Australia in the finals of the 400 meter. The American's time was 5:04.2, while Borg clocked 5:05.6 and Charlton finished at 5:06.6.

"Oh, that was so close!" Dawn said. "You weren't kidding about this being fun."

"One race and one gold medal," Martha added.

The time between the 400 and 1500 meter races was spent chatting about the amazing showing of the USA team's platform and springboard divers. First, the men's team had shocked the world by taking six out of the nine medals being awarded. American women, determined not to be outdone, won five of the six women's diving medals. Only Hjordis Topel of Sweden, who won a bronze medal in the platform, had prevented the American women from a sweep.

The names of previously unknown swimmers like Albert White, David Fall, Clarence Pinkston, and Pete Desjardins were splashed in bold letters across the front pages of newspapers around the world. Elizabeth Becker, Caroline Smith, Aileen Riggin, and Caroline Fletcher transformed themselves from unknown young ladies practicing long lonely hours in high school and college swimming pools into international celebrities. Pretty faces and well formed bodies did nothing to diminish the photographers' enthusiasm or publishers' willingness to print their pictures in newspapers worldwide.

American spectators waited patiently during the twenty-plus minutes it took for Boy Charlton of Australia to win the 1500 meter freestyle. It had become obvious early in the race that the Americans had no one who could compete with other countries in the long distances. Arne Borg of Sweden finished second with Francis Beaurepaire of Australia finishing third. The third place finisher seemed to be a favorite with the crowd, and the American group decided it must be because of his French surname.

American enthusiasm renewed as the crowd cheered on a Hawaiian youngster, Warren Kealoha, to a gold medal in the 100 meter back stroke just ahead of Joseph de Combe of Belgium and another American, Paul Wyatt. More clapping and screaming erupted as Team USA won the four times 200 meter relay a full eight seconds ahead of Australia.

Robert Skelton followed with a gold medal in the 200 meter breaststroke, with teammate William Kirschbaum taking the bronze, and a rout appeared to be underway.

During the next intermission, excitement mounted as everyone in the grandstand waited for the 100 meter freestyle to begin.

Bud glanced over at Dawn as Johnny Weissmuller and the Kahanamoku brothers splashed water on their tall, well-muscled bodies and stretched in preparation for the race that would determine the world's fastest swimmer. "Incredibly fit-looking guys," he remarked.

"Oh really? I hadn't noticed," she responded.

"Liar, liar, pants on fire," Martha teased.

The loudest cheers were saved for this last race of the day as Johnny Weissmuller, Duke Kahanamoku, and Samuel Kahanamoku battled to first-second-and third place finishes ahead of the disappointed Australian and Swedish swimmers. Weissmuller's 59 second race was only 1.4 seconds ahead of Duke's time, and 2.8 eight seconds faster than bronze medal winner, Samuel Kahanamoku.

The final totals for the men's swimming competition was: USA nine medals, Australia four, Sweden three, and Hungary and Belgium each one.

The Southern California contingent was in a jovial mood the next day as they walked to their seats to watch the finals for the women's swim team. Much had been said about how the women divers had been spurred to victory watching the men's team's performance, and now ladies from the United States swim team were determined to also win as many medals as their male counterparts.

Ethel Lackie, Mariechen Wehsellau, and Gertrude Ederle's one, two, three finish in the 100 meters gave the USA team three medals in three tries. When it was followed by Martha Norelius, Helen Wainwright, and Gertrude Ederle's sweep in 400 meter, the American spectators were beside themselves, yelling and slapping each other on the backs.

Next, it was Glenn Hartcranft's turn to jump up and down and yell as his new friend, Sybil Bauer, ran away with the women' 100 meter backstroke beating Phyllis Harding of Great Britain by over four seconds. Harding only took second by eight-tenths of a second ahead of third place finisher, Aileen Riggin of the USA.

British fans finally got to cheer when Lucy Morton won the gold medal in the 200 meter breaststroke, and her British teammate, Gladys Carson, won the bronze. USA's Agnes Geraghty kept American hearts pounding taking second place only eight- tenths of as second behind Morton. USA's girls were not making it easy on other country's competitors.

Women's Team USA took control of the final race, winning the four time 100 meter relay by an astounding 18 1/2 seconds over second place finisher, Great Britain. Fans of all countries stood and applauded the Swedish team as they watched these valiant women swim their hearts out until the very end, in spite finishing a full 37 seconds behind the Americans. Standing poolside, the four Swedish women wore their newly-won bronze medals and smiled as proudly as the gold-medal winners as they listened to the American

National Anthem being played. The Americans had won the race, but the Swedish women had captured everyone's hearts, including Team USA.

At the end of the day, as people began filing out of the grandstands, the Americans had won ten medals, the British four, and the Swedish women one.

Dawn looked away from the celebrating Americans surrounding her toward some stony-faced citizens of other countries and asked, "Do you think winning so much is going to cause us to be disliked by people from other countries?"

Bud answered her question with a question. "How well do you like the California Bears?"

"I hate them."

"I'm glad he didn't ask about Stanford," Glenn Hartcranft said.

"Do you like the Cal Bears?" Dawn asked the Stanford athlete.

"Of course not. What's to like?"

Chapter 36

Bud had experienced difficulty eating breakfast this morning, and now, as he and Swede Anderson approached the shot put ring, he was trying to prevent his stomach from tying into knots. Normally, before any competition, he kept his mind focused on the task at hand. Extraordinary circumstances sometimes call for a change in strategy, and Bud felt this was one of those times. Turning to Swede, he asked, "What do you think about the Brit, Eric Lydell, changing from the 100 meters to the 400 meters because he wouldn't run one of the preliminaries on a Sunday?"

"Didn't Jesus pull a donkey out of the mud on the Sabbath?"

"You're saying he made a mistake?"

Swede shrugged his shoulders. "It was his choice. I just don't get the connection."

"And yet he surprised everyone by winning the gold in the 400, and his teammate, Harold Abrahams, nosed out our guy, Jackson Schultz, in the 100 meters."

"Are you thinking of dropping out of the discus competition this Sunday,"

"No, but I admire Lydell for living up to his convictions."

"Whatever you say, Bud, but don't you think it's time that we should be…"

"Isn't it great Otto and Cliff each won a gold medal in the relays. They were pretty disappointed about not placing in their events."

"Yeah, but it's a shame Leighton was edged out for the bronze in the 110 meter hurdles."

"I believe Leighton feels like it's an honor just to be here."

"I feel the same way myself," Swede confessed. "Now, what would you think about us concentrating on our own event?"

"Good idea."

During the first round, a bad case of nervous tension had caused Thomas Lieb, Glenn Hartcranft, and Swede Anderson to push the 16-pound ball short of the distances they had reached in practice. This resulted in the Finns standing in first, second, and third place. At this point, it looked like the big guys from Finland might be able to pull off another victory similar to the one four years ago. There was no more time for Bud to rid himself of the butterflies in his stomach or the unfamiliar weakness in his knees. It was his turn to enter the ring. He remembered how Helen Wills had put her hands on her knees and taken deep breaths as the players changed sides during her six-two, six-two win in the singles tennis championship. Nothing else he had done had reduced his tension, and he figured it was worth a try. His first throw was far from his best, but it landed just short of Eero Lehtonen's second-place marker, leaving him in third place after the first round.

Bud's effort seemed to inspire some of his teammates, and they began performing closer to their full potential. Glenn Hartcranft unleashed a mighty throw of 48 feet-6 inches followed by Ralph Hills' toss of 48 feet even. Bud felt like he was expending more energy than at any time in his career, but still remained in third place with a toss of 47 feet 10-inches. The pressure of competing in the biggest sports event in the world was causing strong men's hearts to beat wildly.

Finally, it came time for Bud's final throw. The Finns had not been able to match the final distances of Team USA and it looked like another sweep for the Americans. Hartcranft was in first place with his last effort reaching a seemingly insurmountable 48 feet 10 1/4 inches, Hills stood at 48 feet 1/2 inch, and Bud held onto third place at 47 feet-11 inches. Bud looked up toward the sky, took a deep breath, and whispered, "I'm not asking for any special favors, just help me to do the best I can with the ability you've given me." He balanced the shot put on the palm of his right hand, turned around toward the cheering crowd, and glanced up toward the area where Dawn had said she and his sister would be sitting. There was no way to separate them from others in the crowd of over 60,000 people, and yet, somehow, his eyes landed directly on the spot where he could see them jumping up and down and waving at him. His butterflies disappeared, and his legs gained new strength. He crouched low, knowing his spin had to be faster and his release more powerful than ever before. He felt a surge of adrenaline as his body uncoiled, and a yell escaped his lips as he launched the shot put as high and far as gravity allowed.

Bud stood with his head down and his eyes closed as the voice over the loudspeaker proclaimed, "Ladies and gentlemen, if you will direct your attention to the shot put ring Bud Houser of the United States has just set a new Olympic shot put record with a distance of 14.995 meters, or 49 feet 2 1/4 inches." The explosive roar of the stadium crowd sent shock waves through his body, as the fulfillment of a life long dream suddenly became a reality.

*   *   *

All the thrills Bud Houser had experienced during his athletic career paled in comparison to this one moment in time. Standing in the center of the track between teammates Ralph Hills and Glenn Hartcranft with a gold medal draped from a red-white-and-blue ribbon around his neck, and the band playing his country's national anthem, tears steamed freely down his face. He had often heard it said that striving toward one's goal is as exciting as achieving it. While that might be true in some endeavors, being presented with an Olympic gold medal in front of thousands of screaming fans easily surpassed anything that had gone before or that he expected to happen to him anytime in the future.

Chapter 37

"Twenty-four rue-de-la-Grande Truanderie," Dawn told the taxi driver.

The driver tipped back his cap and cocked his head to one side while mentally deciphering the strongly accented directions, and then grinned. "Bistro Pharamond?"

"Whee." Dawn answered.

Only Bud sitting in the front passenger seat could see the Frenchman struggling not to laugh at his passenger's fractured French. "You will enjoy the food at Pharamond," he said in perfect English. "I would recommend either the veal or the fresh sea scallops, but don't leave without trying one of their desserts."

"You speak English," Martha said.

The driver reached in his shirt pocket and handed a business card back over his shoulder. "I graduated from Redondo Beach High School. Just call me 10 minutes ahead, and I'll be at your hotel door." He glanced over at Bud, who was sitting in the seat that he felt should be the driver's, nervously watching the taxi maneuver down the avenue. "My name is Louie Jean LaMonde. I guess you're celebrating your big victory today."

"That's right. My fiancée and sister are taking me to dinner. Were you at the games?"

"I heard the news on the radio before I came to work."

Dawn said, "I've seen a lot of local people in our hotel lobby listening to the Olympics on the radio, but I haven't seen as many in the grandstands."

"It's because they're at different events. "France won four gold medals in cycling, and the French team dominated all the fencing events. Our biggest heroes over here are cyclist Roger Ducret, and gymnastics star, Albert Sequin. There is some controversy about the way the points are counted. The United States is way ahead for first place in the track and field events, but some over here feel France should be in second place."

"I've heard about that," Bud said. "France has won more medals than Finland, yet is still in third place."

"I guess either country can stake their claim. Up until now, we have two more total medals, but Finland has one more gold."

"Henri Cochet gave our guy, Vincent Richards, all he could handle in the tennis singles finals."

"Still, France took three silvers in tennis while the United States took all five golds."

"Do you feel torn about which team to support?"

Louie Jean smiled. "Don't tell anyone, but I'm happy when either team wins."

"Just our luck," Dawn whispered to Martha. "We had to get an English-speaking taxi driver when Bud is in the front seat."

The taxi pulled up to the restaurant, and a doorman helped Dawn and Martha out of the automobile.

Martha looked at the potted plants, green awning and crystal-windowed door, and said, "If the interior of the restaurant is as elegant as the entrance, this should be a night to remember."

"You ain't seen nothin' yet," Louie Jean promised.

The doorman had no idea the English words the taxi driver had spoken were grammatically incorrect and wondered why everyone was laughing.

Dawn counted out what seemed to Bud like too many francs. "We'll call you from now on whenever we need a taxi."

"Thanks. Have a nice dinner."

Chapter 38

With only a few more events to be held, the 1924 Olympics would soon be history. Some athletes were already packing their suitcases, and preparations were in the final stages for the closing ceremony. Winners in the hammer throw and discus were still to be decided, and the 3000 meter race was currently underway. Participants in the discus throw were on the field, but most of them were weighing the benefits of warming up against the disadvantage of tiring themselves out. During the last couple of days, Paris's normally mild weather had transformed itself into a sweltering heat.

"That's all the warm-up I can handle," Swede Anderson announced. "My shirt is soaking wet, to say nothing about my socks."

Bud pulled the front of his wet shirt away from his body and shook it up and down several times. "Who told us that summers in Paris weren't too hot?"

"I heard that only 15 runners out of the 38 that started the 10,000 meter cross-country yesterday finished the race, and some of those men had to be taken to the hospital."

"Yet, Paavo Nurmi won his fourth gold medal in five days. I don't know what was tougher for him, winning the 1500 meter and 5,000 meter within an hour of each other or winning the 10,000 meter yesterday in the heat. It's amazing one man can have such a huge heart."

"What do you want to bet he'll be leading the pack when they come in for the finish of the 3,000 meter?" Swede asked.

"If you give me 50 to 1 odds, I might risk a dollar on that," Bud answered.

"Too late, here he comes."

They stopped and watched the man they called, "The Flying Finn," run through the gate, go around the track once, and then cross the finish line just as some of the other runners were entering the stadium. An amazing climax to the Finn's Olympic performance and today he had won his race in 113 degree heat. The American and Finnish spectators cheered loudly, while much of the crowd clapped politely.

"Five gold medals for that guy. I guess that was the final nail in the coffin for France's chance at finishing second in the track events," Swede observed.

"Talk about a giant killer, that guy doesn't look any bigger than Dawn."

"5 foot 2 and 112 pounds," Swede confirmed.

Glenn Hartcranft came up to join the two Trojans. "Wow, have you ever seen weather this hot?"

Bud started to tell his friendly competitors about the intense heat during the summers he'd worked in Corcoran, and then decided it might be wise to keep that information to himself. He let his mind wander back.....

*   *   *

Digging deep into the pocket of his faded blue jeans, Bud pulled out his worn railroad watch. It was 10 minutes before 4:00. A little over two more hours of loading 100 pound hay bales onto trucks and he could call it a day. Just a few more weeks and he could go back home to Oxnard. 45 cents an hour, five days a week had put some nice change in his pocket for the next school year, but the real reason he was doing this was to build his strength and toughness for the weight events at Oxnard High School.

Some locals had told him that the 108 degrees the temperature had reached last week was as hot as it ever got in Corcoran. They were wrong. Pushing his left fist into the aching spot in the middle of his back, he flicked the sweat off his forehead with his right hand. He remembered the lifeguard position he'd been offered and wondered what the effect would have been if he had taken advantage of that opportunity and spent his spare time practicing the shot put and discus.

"Hey, come on Buddy. These bales aren't going to load themselves."

Sinking a hay hook into each side of another bale, he lifted it quickly to waist high, and then let his knee and arms combine to push it the rest of the way onto the truck bed. Just above the right knee, his skin showed through his jeans from the thousands of bales he had already loaded this summer.

After a dozen more bales, the knarled older man asked, "You about ready to switch places?"

Bud took a of couple quick steps forward, slapped both hands on the truck bed, and swung himself up to a standing position next to his co-worker.

"I wish I could still do that," the older man said.

*　　　*　　　*

"I wish I could still do that."

"Wish you could still do what?" Swede asked.

"Oh, never mind. I guess I was thinking out loud."

"Are you okay, Buddy? The heat isn't getting to you, is it?"

Bud laughed. "You know, I think I'm going to be just fine."

Fourth place in many track meets earned you a medal, but not in the Olympics. After just missing a bronze medal in the shot put, Swede Anderson started out the day with a tremendous heave of 146 feet 11 inches. In this heat, and considering all the pressure the athletes were under, this throw looked like it gave him an excellent chance at winning a medal.

Thomas Lieb had not won a medal yesterday and was equally as frustrated. The officials marked his first throw at an even one 147 feet, putting him one heartbreaking inch longer than Swede's distance. At least it was heartbreaking for the big Trojan. The Finns were not ready to give up their former superiority that easily. With the two American markers to shoot for, Vilho Niittymaa sailed the discus out to 147 feet 5 inches. It was now apparent to both the crowd and the athletes that, in spite of the heat, a sub-par performance would not be enough to win any medals today.

Glenn Hartcranft and Ralph Hills seemed less able to cope with the blazing sun and left their tosses short of the others. After winning the silver and bronze in the shot put, neither man seemed as disappointed as Bud's friend Swede Anderson.

Bud's first toss traveled just two inches short of the Finn's, leaving him in second place.

The heat began catching up with the athletes as all the participants sent their second and third shots short of their first distance. With only Bud's final toss still to go, and the athletes in various states of heat exhaustion, it appeared that Niittymaa had won the gold, with Bud taking the silver, and Thomas Lieb winning the bronze. Bud once again turned and faced the stands. The spot where Dawn and Martha had told him to look was a sea of red-white-and blue, and it seemed everyone was waving and cheering. That was okay. He knew they were there. Crouching low, he visualized his body as a tight spring getting ready to uncoil. As soon as the saucer left his hand, he knew what he had done. Watching it fly high through the air, he muttered, "Thank God for those summers in Corcoran."

"Ladies and gentlemen, if you will look toward the discus ring, Bud Houser of the USA has won his second gold medal of this Olympics with a toss of 46.115 meters, or for you Americans 151 feet 4 inches. The silver medalist is Vilho Niittymaa of Sweden, with Thomas Lieb of the USA taking home the bronze."

Bud looked toward the spot where he knew his fiancée and sister would be hugging each other and celebrating, but could only see hundreds of fans jumping up and down. The enormity of what he had done caused him to fall to his knees.

Bud felt his emotions had been toughened by the awarding of the gold medal in the shot put, but when the band started playing the "Star Spangled Banner" again, the tears again fell unabated.

Swede put his arm over Bud's shoulder as they walked toward the locker room. "I'm proud of you, my friend. You're only a sophomore at USC, and you've already won two Olympic gold medals. Who knows how far you're going to fling the discus or put the shot when you grow up?"

"And I'll be just as proud of you when I'm sitting in the stands watching you and the Trojan Varsity kick the hell out of the Cal Bears next year."

"If you're sitting in the stands, it will be by choice. You know how badly Howard Jones wants you on the team."

*   *   *

During the final Parade of Nations, Bud again had to grit his teeth and rapidly blink his eyes as his team marched past French President Domerque while the band began playing the national anthem. Due to his unprecedented feat of being the only man to ever win both the shot put and discus at the same Olympics, Bud had been given the honor of carrying the American flag and leading Team USA around the track. He and his teammates wore the same white pants, navy coats, and red, white and blue ties that they had worn during the opening ceremonies, but as they removed their straw hats and faced the grandstands, a new pride showed on their faces. These young men and women had demonstrated to the world that their country was a powerful force in international athletics. After American Colonel, Robert E. Thompson, officially accepted the team awards, the Prince of Wales left his seat, walked out onto the field, and began congratulating the victorious Americans. It was a moment in time that the members of the 1924 United States Olympic team would never forget.

Marching just behind Bud, Leyton Dye asked, "Do you think you'll go to the 1928 Olympics in Amsterdam?"

"Hopefully I'll have my hands full with my dental practice by then." Bud answered.

"This is just a rumor," Cliff Argue remarked, "but I hear they might even allow dentists to compete by then."

While keeping his eyes focused ahead as he walked, Bud said. "Beating the Cal-Bears, and winning the national championship in track for USC, is only a few months off. It's hard for me to think ahead to 1928."

From another row behind them Otto Anderson said, "My wife tells me Holland would be a great place for a second honeymoon."

Bud's eyes widened.

Chapter 39

Members of the victorious 1924 United States Olympic team were transformed from obscurity to instant celebrity, but none more than Bud Houser. The handsome young giant-killer became a symbol of pride for the American public. One reporter quoted Bud as saying he had begun throwing large rocks while he was still a boy. Now, youngsters from New York to California began competing with each other pushing heavy stones and flinging makeshift discuses in farms, back yards, and vacant lots throughout the land. The less fortunate around the country were assured that no matter how humble their beginnings, they could rise above their circumstances. Depictions of Bud's accomplishments went from sports sections to front pages. For an orphan from Winigan, Missouri, now just beginning his junior year at the University of Southern California, it was quite overwhelming. The lesson he had learned from Jim Thorpe helped him maintain his humility. In a few years he could either be a former athlete, regaling other farm workers with stories about his past, or a successful dentist, providing an affluent lifestyle for Dawn and their children. He knew his professors at dental school would not make any allowances for his accomplishments in Paris.

Along with increased fame came invitations to speak at various prestigious functions as well as to perform. The fast approaching fall semester at USC forced him to turn down all European invitations with the exception of one track meet in Great Britain.

With all speculations about whether Bud would win the Olympics resolved, rumors about when and where he would wed the beautiful coed traveling with him escalated.

*   *   *

"Is my wife here?" Bud asked while holding up a newspaper to his sister Martha.

She opened the hotel room door wider for him to enter. "Let me see that."

"If it's on the front page of the London Times, it must be true," he added.

"BUD HOUSER TAKES BRIDE AFTER GAMES IN PARIS," Martha read.

"If you two start acting like you're married, I'll take a stick to both of you."

"All I know is what I read. Is Dawn ready for church?"

"I'll be right out," Dawn called from the bathroom.

*   *   *

Bud and Dawn had each grown up hearing verbose ministers of the gospel, but were not prepared for the back-to-back sermons delivered this morning at Westminster Abbey.

When H.D.A. Major D.D., the principal of Ripon Hall at Oxford, had concluded his message, the congregation stood to their feet and sang three hymns. Bud and Dawn assumed that Archdeacon R.H. Charles had approached the pulpit to pronounce the benediction, and were surprised when he plunged into another full length sermon. Apparently people of Great Britain were more accustomed to the lengthy gospel messages because no one squirmed to quite the extent as the two young Americans.

"Hold still you two," Martha scolded.

From out of nowhere a loud growling noise disturbed the reverent scene. A few people turned around in their pews and smiled. After all, this young man had treated them to a splendid performance at the USA vs. British Empire track meet yesterday at Stamford Bridge. He couldn't help it if his stomach was demanding to be fed, although most worshipers around him felt that a genteel British citizen would not have allowed such an improper incident to have happened in church.

*   *   *

"Finally," Bud said as he sank his fork into a large piece of unidentified pan-fried fish on his platter of fish and chips.

"How much do you weigh now?" Martha asked.

"One-hundred eighty-two; I'm still down about six pounds from my surgery."

"What your favorite memory since we left Paris?" Dawn asked.

"Seeing the beautiful countryside on the train through France," Martha said. "I'll never forget the battlefields from the World War, but the realization of what took place there was not pleasant."

Bud said, "How about when Dawn crawled into the German foxhole? Lucky for the Germans that none of them were still in there."

She doubled up her fist at him.

"See what I mean?"

Dawn said, "I feel like I got my fill of sightseeing in Paris, but I'll never forget the tower where Joan of Arc was held prisoner and where she died; how about you, Bud?"

"The Trocadero at Picadilly Circus was hard to beat."

"I might have known you'd pick something where food was involved. Well, our ship sails out tomorrow," Martha reminded them. "Are you two about ready to go home?"

"I'll feel better when I know my dad came through his tests okay," Dawn said.

"Don't you think they would have sent us a telegram if they found anything seriously wrong?" Bud asked.

"Knowing my dad, he wouldn't have wanted to spoil our fun."

Chapter 40

Bud answered the louder-than-expected knock on the door to his room at the Astor Hotel in New York.

Dawn came in waving a copy of *Mercury Magazine* in front of his face and stomping her foot. "This is no longer funny. Every time a reporter writes another article like this, I imagine my parents thinking I lied to them."

Bud chuckled, took the magazine from her hand, and began reading. "'An Exclusive Report from Henry Louis Mencken – In a small chapel near Barbizon Village outside of Paris, two time gold medal winner, Bud Houser, exchanged vows with USC art student, Dawn Evelyn Smith. Nothing needs to be said about the bride's personal beauty just look at the accompanying picture. The new Mrs. Houser is the daughter of Dr. and Mrs. Smith of Los Angeles, California. The happy couple will be resuming classes at the University of Southern California this fall.' Mr. Mencken says you are beautiful."

"Yeah, I missed that part. I guess I can send Dad and Mom another telegram. Are you going to wear your dark blue suit again tonight?"

"Of course. It's the only suit I own. I never thought I would say this, but I'm actually getting tired of all these steak dinners they're serving us."

"Maybe the Hotel Astor will have something different. I hear everyone of any importance will be at the Victorious America Celebration."

"That's what they said about the parade down Fifth Avenue. The past month has been the most exciting time of my life, but I can't wait to get home and have things settled down."

Dawn laughed. "You really think the people back home are going to put on less of a celebration for you?"

"Oh boy; I guess not. At least we'll be at home in our own beds. Speaking of beds, I'm getting tired of staying in separate hotel rooms, especially now that Martha has gone home."

"What are you suggesting?"

"Nothing really. How long do you think it will be before we're home?"

"Let's see; a couple of days to Sellersville, spend three of four days there with my parents, and then three days on the train to Los Angeles."

"Back on campus in a little over a week, and then we go from being together constantly to you living over on Pico Boulevard and me at the Sigma Chi house."

"I guess that's the plan."

He took a step closer and took both of her hands. "After being with you almost constantly since the end of the Games, I can't stand the thought of going back to just seeing you on weekends and the evenings neither of us has to study."

"What are you proposing?"

"We need to be living together, eating together, and sleeping together…"

Her face turned crimson, and she took a step back. "Bud, I could never do anything like that."

He pulled her toward him. "What I'm saying is, we need to get married just as soon as we get home."

"But we said we would wait until the middle of our senior year."

"Do you really want to wait that long?"

She came into his arms, and her feet left the floor in a slow twirling dance. I don't think I can wait that long either."

"Why are you out of breath when I'm the one doing the lifting?" he asked.

"Why are you breathing so hard when I only weigh 114 pounds?"

Chapter 41

December 5, 1924

Sitting alone in the kitchen of the tiny cottage located in back of her parent's house, Dawn opened the partially-filled scrapbook and arranged the newspaper and magazine clippings lying on the table. A small Christmas tree sat on a table by the window. It was all she and Bud needed. Christmas morning would be celebrated near the huge Christmas tree that stood in her parents' house in the same spot as it had been every year as far back as she could remember. The overhead light illuminated the headlines and most of the copy well enough, but she needed a magnifying glass to read some of the small print. She had nearly finished the fourth sixteen-by-eleven inch scrapbook in front of her and wondered how many more there would be before her husband's athletic career ended.

Before their marriage, Dawn imagined herself and Bud spending more time having fun and indulging in romantic activities. His need to practice throwing the shot put and discus after classes on most afternoons, and studying almost every night reserved those moments for weekends. She looked forward to movies, church, going to the beach or the mountains, and loving interludes before starting another long week. She had her own art assignments, but enjoyed the reminiscing involved when pasting her husband's pictures and news clippings. She kept a smaller brown, leather scrapbook of her own, filed with dance cards, ticket stubs, menus, and other nostalgic paraphernalia. If their future kids didn't know all about their parents' younger life, it would be because they just didn't make the effort.

Because of Bud's fame throughout the country, her father had arranged for friends from around the country to mail clippings from the New York Times, the Chicago Tribune, and other cities where articles about Bud would have otherwise been missed. Pasting those, along with magazine clippings and articles from the Los Angeles newspapers, consumed at least one full evening each week. The actual work could have been accomplished faster, but her curiosity demanded that she read through everything at least once.

She chuckled as she looked at a glossy sketch of a young man studying, while the bubble above his head showed a huge home and what looked like a brand new Studebaker. "That's my sweetheart," she said.

"Did you call me?" Bud's voice came from the bed-room.

"No, just thinking out loud she called back. Sorry I interrupted your studies."

One more look at the sketch confirmed that, while the idea was good, if she had drawn it, the character would have been much more interesting. Her artistic sense caused her to create a proper balance for each page. She placed the cartoon at the bottom left of the page, and then she picked out a large clipping. By spacing out stories and pictures about their romance and wedding, she could slip them into the books without destroying the integrity of her husband's achievements. Looking at the eight-inch full-body shot of Bud holding the shot put in one hand while the other stretched out in front of him, she decided it was one of her favorites. His track suit with its short shorts showed off his physique and made her squirm a little. Her picture, just to right of his, showed only her face and hand. The headline read, "Paris? No. Los Angeles!" The copy above read, "Miss Dawn Evelyn Smith (Bushnell photo) new wife of Clarence 'Bud' Houser (International Newsreel photo), two-time Olympic gold medal winner passed up the 'Fashion Capital' for home city for nuptials." After carefully pasting the clipping in the top center, she read the copy below. "Five years ago Dawn Smith peeked through a knothole in the fence surrounding Housh Field at Los Angeles High School. For the first time, she saw Bud Houser, who was then competing in a high school track meet. She arranged an introduction from a cousin in Oxnard. Last night their romance culminated when the couple were married at the home of the bride's parents, Dr. and Mrs. C.C. Smith, 4104 West Pico Street. In the intervening five years, Bud Houser has developed from a star high school athlete into the world's champion discus thrower and shot putter. Coach Dean Cromwell of the University of Southern California attended, along with 20 members of his team. The bridegroom is a student at the USC Dental College. The bride is taking art courses at the same institution." So what if the reporter had confused the location of the wedding with the reception; the pictures looked great.

She looked out the window at the grass in the lighted back yard and remembered how the man who stood calmly while bigger men's knees were shaking had looked so frightened when she walked down the aisle of the Pico Avenue Christian Church and met him at the altar. He might have found the strength to carry her over the threshold of their honeymoon cabin on the lake at Lake Arrowhead had she not said, "I'll race you to the bedroom."

She decided that, with all of the pages about his athletic exploits, it wouldn't hurt to devote one page strictly to their wedding, and pasted in a small article titled, "Bud Houser Weds L.A. Girl," another that headlined, "Trojan Track Star to Wed," and the last, "Bud Houser Takes Bride." There were several more articles about the wedding, but she had to pick and choose.

The picture of the Los Angeles Coliseum was so wide it barely fit across the top of the next page. The headline across the top read, "43,000 See Bud Houser Set World Record in Discus – Yurmi of Finland Sets Record in 3 Mile Run."

When it was neatly in place, she recalled how he had explained all of these records to her.

"No, you don't understand. I set an Olympic record in the shot put, not a world's record. The world's record that I set in the discus was broken by Glenn Hartcranft, and then last week when I tossed the discus 156 feet 13 1/2 inches, I broke Glenn's record."

"Then what are all those trophies you have that say, 'world's record?'"

"A lot of them are high school world's records, and others are when I broke someone else's record before someone else broke mine."

"And Leighton Dye has the world record for the high hurdles?"

"No, our friend Leighton holds the Pacific Coast record in the hurdles."

She remembered how he had laughed at the confused look on her face, and then suddenly he grabbed her and kissed her.

After pasting in two more clippings about the track meet with Yurmi, she still had a small empty space at the bottom. She sorted through the stack and found a small clipping that read, "Dental Fraternity Hosts Sport Dance. Delta Sigma Delta is entertaining Friday evening with a sports dance at Wilshire Country Club. Bud Houser of Olympic and local fame is to be guest of honor."

She was just smoothing out the last clipping when her mother came bursting into the kitchen.

"Come quick! It's your father! He's closed his eyes, and I can't wake him up!"

Bud was out the door and running toward the main house before Dawn could get out of her chair. He found his father-in-law slumped awkwardly in his leather chair.

"Dad! Dad! Can you hear me?

Dr. Smith opened his eyes and said, "That's the first time you have ever called me Dad."

Dawn came running up to her father's chair followed closely by her mother. Her father's gray pallor frightened her. "What's the matter, Dad?"

Dr. Smith raised his hand up to his chest. "It feels like I have a heavy weight right here."

"Get some cold towels," Cora said. "Bud, you call an ambulance."

Chapter 42

The trio in the hospital waiting room sat silently, each consumed with their own thoughts and prayers.

"I've been Mrs. C.C. Smith ever since I was a girl," Cora thought. "What if he doesn't make it? It would be like losing part of me. An empty house. An empty bed. I don't even remember what my life was like before him. God, please don't let him die, or if he does go, please take me too. I don't want to be a widow."

Dawn stared into space. "Dad was always the strong one. How could this be happening to him? He was always in control, always had the right answer for each problem; always found something positive in even the toughest situations. I haven't even opened all of my wedding gifts yet, and what would Christmas be like if wasn't here? He's always been there smiling and being more interested in what other people were receiving than in any gifts he opened for himself. Please God, don't take my father. Not now. Not yet."

Memories of Bud's mother became more vivid to him than they had been in years. "I was no more than a toddler when she died, yet somehow I can remember her picking me up and holding me in her arms. I can remember myself at nine years old climbing into the hayloft in Winigan, Missouri and crying over the loss of my father. This can't be happening again. It just can't be happening. Martha's husband has been a surrogate father to me since I was just a kid climbing off the train in Oxnard, but Dr. Smith is my mentor, the man I most want to be like. He's the one who had inspired me to go to dental college. I've always been suspicious that he engineered Jim Thorpe coming out to Bovard Field to convince me that passing my courses in dental school was more important than playing football. How like Dr. Smith that would be. Maybe he could have been convincing enough, but with his friend, Jim Thorpe, in town, why not show me an example of what it would be like to devote my life to sports and hardly be able to support my family. And now this wonderful man is just beyond this wall struggling for his life. God, give the doctor special skills. We aren't ready to let him go."

The grim look on the Dr. Thomas's face brought tears to everyone's eyes before he ever said a word. He turned to Cora. "I'm sorry, Mrs. Smith. Your husband was a close friend of mine. We did everything we could. His heart just gave out." The doctor paused for a moment as Cora absorbed the news, and then said, "Why don't we all go into the chapel?"

Cora put her face in her hands as sobs shook her whole body and a pitiful wailing sound escaped from her lips.

Dawn wiped the tears from her face, but more tears immediately replaced them as she wept.

Bud put one arm around his grief-stricken wife and the other around his suffering mother-in-law and made no attempt to stifle his own tears.

All three followed the doctor into the small chapel and up to a picture of Jesus looking compassionately down on them.

"He didn't hear our prayers," Dawn sobbed.

"Oh, He heard them," the doctor said. "There are tears in his eyes too."

Chapter 43

June 1926

Dawn answered the doorbell and greeted Yale Martz and his new wife, the former Margaret Hill. "Did you have any trouble finding our new house?"

"No, the directions you gave us were perfect," Margaret said.

"Where is Dr. Houser?" Yale asked.

Dawn laughed, "I don't know if he's ready to be called that yet. He's still exhausted from the board exams. A quiet night out with old friends is just what we need. Why all the mystery about where we're going to eat?"

"Congratulations Miss 'Most Popular Girl on Campus'," Bud said as he walked into the living room.

"And congratulations to you, 'Mr. Most Popular Man'," Margaret replied.

"Do you think these two need to be alone so they can break their arms patting themselves on the back?" Dawn asked Yale.

"Hey! If only men were allowed to vote, you would have won hands down," Margaret said. "You're just too pretty to get the women's vote."

"Where are we going to eat?" Bud asked. "I'm starved."

"You will know when we get there," Yale said.

"Okay, my friend; I really don't care where we eat as long as I get a seat close to a waiter."

After 20 minutes on the road, it became obvious to Bud and Dawn that Yale wasn't heading toward any restaurant in Los Angeles.

"If we're going to eat in Oxnard, I might have to stop at some diner and grab a sandwich," Bud complained.

"Actually, there is this great restaurant in Ventura we've wanted to take you to." Yale teased.

Finally Yale wheeled the car up to the curb in front of the Greenwich Village Café inside the Christy Hotel in Hollywood. A big sandwich board out front read, "BUD HOUSER NIGHT, Collegiate Dancing Contest for Bud Houser Trophy. Bud Houser Will Present Trophy in Person. Wanda Hathaway Review with Harry Cook in 'College Humor,' Eddie Bergstrom Paramount Collegiate Band."

Bud placed the heel of his hand on his forehead, closed his eyes, and sighed.

"Sorry, Bud," Yale said. "I was just assigned to get you here."

"He will love it once we get inside," Dawn said. "Besides, honey, you don't have to wear a necktie tonight."

As soon as he heard the band playing "Fight On" as they entered the combination dinner-theater and dance hall, Bud knew this wasn't going to be another stuffy banquet with dignitaries making long, boring speeches. As the crowd stood and cheered, he glanced around and discovered that, even though the crowd numbered close to 200, he saw familiar faces at almost every table. Looking to the left, he saw a group of celebrities, including Johnny Weissmuller and Buster Crabbe, who were with him at the Olympics in Paris. The rest of the hall contained members of the track and football teams, Sigma Chi brothers, coaches, professors, and even a few of Dawn's Delta Gamma sisters and their dates. As he was being escorted to a table down in front, he greeted Leighton Dye and his wife, Eleanor, Otto Anderson and his wife, Hazel Bobbitt Anderson, and Coaches Dean Cromwell, Gus Henderson, and Howard Jones.

The applause didn't subside until the Housers and Martzs were seated, after which his old friend Swede Anderson came over, gave him a hug that almost caused him to fall off his chair, and made his way to the bandstand.

"Fellow Trojans, and all of you friends of Bud, I've prepared a four-hour tribute to my great friend, after which you will all be served dinner." He waited until all of the hooting and groaning had ended, and then he began. "It's interesting that I would be the one to recite Bud's exploits seeing that, if it wasn't for him, I would have won a ton more medals in the shot put and discus while I was at USC. Ever since Bud Houser was in high school, we have followed his athletic achievements in newspapers, magazines, and on the newsreel. We even watched him playing himself in a Hollywood movie. Tonight I'm going to tell you many things you already know, because they are worthy of repeating, and I'll cover some other things you probably don't know. Bud burst onto the national scene when he beat Olympic champion, Pat McDonald, in the shot put while he was still a junior in high school, and the national press has hounded him ever since that day. He would have you believe it was because of his athletic accomplishments, but we all know it was because of his movie star good looks. To give you an idea of what kind of athlete the town's newest dentist is, in one high school track meet, he set a national high school record in the shot put, and then for an afterthought won the discus, the 100 yard dash, the 120 yard high hurdles, and the high jump. Of course, even Bud can't win them all. He was only able to take second place in the 440. Could it be possible he was a little tired by that time? Bud and his high school buddy, Cliff Argue, were the only two members of the Oxnard track team to enter the Southern California High School Championships, and they won first place. The following year Bud went to the national championships, entered six events, and won second place all by himself. Was he a one man track team? You tell me. The fact that he has always competed against guys about six times his size in the weight events hasn't hurt his reputation either. In the 1924 Olympics, he was the first man to ever win gold medals in both the shot put and the discus. Strong men often get weak in the knees when they are under pressure. I know as well as anyone that there is no greater pressure than competing against this guy who refuses to be beat. If I were to try and recite all of his high school records, Pacific Coast records, AAU records, Olympic records, and world's records, many of which he himself broke again, I actually *would* be up here for four hours. Bud led the Trojans to back-to- back track national championships in 1925 and 1926, and just this year," Swede paused and looked around the crowd, "led the mighty Trojans to an 89 to 49 humiliation of our long-time nemesis, the California Bears." He waited as the crowd erupted in applause. "You all remember the speculation about whether Bud would marry his beautiful girlfriend while they were in Paris. Well, I'm not normally one to take the credit, but if I had a nickel for every time I stopped them from marching down the aisle." He paused again while members of the audience wagged their fingers at Bud and Dawn. "Now difficult as this is, I'm going to tell you where my friend, Bud, went so terribly wrong. Many of you don't know this, but while in high school, Bud led Oxnard to league championships in every sport. In fact, the first person to contact him about attending school at Southern California was our former football coach, Elmer 'Gloomy Gus', Henderson. Stand up Coach so everyone can see the man responsible for Bud becoming a Trojan." Coach Henderson stood to his feet and waved to the cheering crowd. "Bud checked to make sure that the university had good coaches in every sport before he chose USC over almost every other college in the nation. Yes, believe me, they all wanted our Buddy. Now here is the sad part; somewhere along the way, Bud lost his sense of priorities. Instead of playing every sport, he chose instead to concentrate on Dental school merely to provide an affluent life after college for his future wife and their children. He could have easily starred in every sport. Well, Bud, I guess no one is perfect, but since you were recently voted the 'Greatest Trojan of All Time' we will forgive you for not helping us go to the Rose Bowl every year you were here. Bud's career at USC has come to an end, however, I've heard directly from Dawn that she wants to go to Amsterdam for a second honeymoon in 1928.

So move over Europe, Bud Houser is coming back again." Swede reached down and lifted his wine glass off the table. Those close to Swede's table could see his eyes were moist as he made his toast. "Here's to the best athlete I have ever seen, and one of the greatest friends a man could ever have. If I had to get beat by someone, at least I was beat by the best in the world. One more thing, for you who are running the dance contest later this evening, don't let Bud enter, because if you do, he will win. Bud come up here and say a few words."

As Bud rose from his chair and headed toward the bandstand, he remembered how terrified he had been when asked to speak at his graduation and presentation of the new Bud Houser athletic field in Oxnard. Years of speaking at large gatherings, both in the United States and abroad had given him the ability to be at ease in front of large crowds.

"Well, you certainly pulled one on me tonight. Yale and Margaret told me they were taking my sweet wife and I out for a quiet dinner someplace. But, now that I'm here, there is no place in the world that I would rather be than with all my friends here at..." He turned to Dawn, "Where are we Honey? Yes, of course, the Greenwich Village Café. Now you know who has the brains in our family. Anyway, it's hard to believe that it's been four years since I first walked down fraternity row and was greeted by a Sigma Chi member who invited me to lunch at his fraternity house. At that lunch, I first heard the phrase, 'Once a Trojan, always a Trojan.' It wasn't long until I found out how true that statement is." Bud waited until the cheers died down. "While it would be foolish to deny that I've accomplished most of the goals I set for myself before arriving at USC, the friends I have made while at the university are of equal importance. You guys and gals will be friends for the rest of my life." He waited again for the cheering to subside. "As for winning national championships the last couple years, how could we lose with guys like Leighton Dye and Ken Grumbles setting records in the high and low hurdles, Lee Barnes winning the pole vault in every meet, and our sprinters and relay teams running away from all their competition. Stand up you guys on the track team, and let everyone get a look at the national champs." Bud singled out Lee Barnes and said, "Let's hear a cheer for the guy who won the Olympic pole vault in 1924 while he was still at Hollywood High School." When the noise began to die down, Bud continued. "My good friend, Swede Anderson, minimized his own career while at USC. He did beat me a few times in the weight events and made me work like crazy to win a lot of others. Competition from him helped me to always be at my best. He was also one of the toughest men to ever play tackle for the University of Southern California Varsity. While he was playing for the Trojans, our team won an unbelievable 25 games against only five losses. He played 60 minutes of every game, and it was common knowledge among opposing teams that if you tried to run off right tackle when USC was on defense, you were going down. There are quite a bunch of us who won't be around next year. Ken, Leighton, Swede, Otto, and I will be trying to make our college educations pay off out in the business world, but Coach Cromwell tells me he might have the best freshman class arriving in the history of the school, and Coach Howard Jones has the most talented high school players on the Pacific Coast lining up to play for him at the Los Angeles Coliseum. I've heard a rumor that Coach Jones is talking to Knute Rockne of Notre Dame about starting a series of home and home games between the two schools. If that happens that will become the greatest rivalry in the history of college football. Well, I thought Swede was long winded. I imagine all of you are anxious to get some food in your stomach and begin the dance contest and show to follow. What Swede said about me winning the dance contest is not true. All you have to do is ask Dawn. I'm lucky to get off the dance floor without breaking something." The crowd laughed as Dawn nodded her head vigorously.

Chapter 44

October 8, 1927

Seeing the way Bud was looking at her as she walked across the bedroom, Dawn ducked under his outstretched arm, grabbed her cardinal light weight wool sweater, and pulled it on over her head. "The luncheon starts in just over an hour, and it's supposed to be another 'Bud Houser Day.'"

"I'm ready to go," he said.

"Yeah, I can see that."

"I meant to the luncheon and football game. You would think that, now that the 1927 football season has started, track and field would be old news."

"The public doesn't soon forget its heroes, sweetheart."

As overwhelming as the attention Bud had received after the 1924 Olympics had been, the longevity of his celebrity status seemed even more remarkable. It had been over three years since his two gold medals in the 1924 Olympics, but Bud's habit of setting new world records and helping win national championships at USC had fanned the flames. The USC Athletic Department hosted a dinner the night after Bud's graduation, and Coach Dean Cromwell presented him with a gold watch upon which was inscribed "The Greatest Trojan of All Time." Following that, the Los Angeles Athletic Club put on their own dinner presenting him with a trophy inscribed "Southern California Athlete of the Year," with a large oil painting of him to later be hung in their lounge.

Award dinners finally began to die down, and Bud and Dawn settled into a pleasant routine. He began building his dental practice, and they filled their leisure time with church activities, dinners out with old friends, and occasional weekends in Lake Arrowhead or Palm Springs. One day a letter arrived from Eldon Snow, a man who had been in Bud's graduating class. It explained that the graduating class of 1926 had picked Eldon to chair a committee sponsoring "Bud Houser Day." It would begin with a luncheon in the new student union building prior to the USC/ Oregon State football game and progress to a reserved section on the 50 yard line of the Coliseum. Because Bud and Dawn had never missed a Trojan home game since they were freshman at the university, and Bud was now adept at public speaking, it was an honor that should require little effort on his part.

The most interesting part of the letter was that they were asking each member of Bud's graduating class to contribute one dollar which would purchase their lunch, and their ticket to the game. A gold ring for Bud would be purchased with the surplus proceeds. Bud had more medals and trophies than Dawn could find shelves on which to place them or wall space to hang them, but a gold ring was something he could enjoy.

*   *   *

"I like being in the alumni section on this side of the field," Dawn said. "We get a little bit of sun, and then in a little while, we'll be in the shade."

Bud looked down at the ring on the third finger of his right hand and moved it back and forth to see the gold sparkle in the sun.

"You really like that ring, don't you?"

"Isn't it great the way the gold figure slinging the discus stands out on the cardinal onyx?"

"And they made it to look just like you. Eldon said our senior class president, Barton Hutchins, designed it himself and then had a jewelry maker copy the design. I'm sure they used a picture of you. It was a great idea giving you something you can use instead of another trophy to try and find a place for. Still, I'm glad you're the one wearing it. It would be much too heavy for me."

Today USC and Oregon State were both undefeated, but local sportswriters claimed that the Beavers would be no match for the Trojans. If "no match" meant the Trojans would finally pull the game out by a score of 13 to 12, the scribes had figured it exactly right.

As they walked toward their usual hangout on Figueroa Avenue, Dawn said, "I love close games like that. They're so exciting."

"I'm exhausted," Bud said. "Not quite this exciting would be fine with me."

"It's no wonder you're so tired. You almost pushed me off my seat every time Oregon State has a good run toward the peristyle end of the field, and then you leaned as far the other way when they were running toward the closed end of the coliseum. Do you think you're actually helping our guys that way?"

He laughed. "You would be surprised how much farther I can make the discus go with the right body-language."

"I'm sure."

The noise was almost deafening as they walked into the eatery and back to the table where their "gang" met to celebrate every Trojan victory and to moan and complain on the rare times when they lost. The small establishment had been called the *"Gag and Barf"* by students and alumni for so many years, no one could remember the restaurant's real name. Yale and Margaret and Leighton and Eleanor already had frosty mugs of beer in front of them, and Otto and Hazel walked in right behind Bud and Dawn.

"Isn't Swede joining us?" Bud yelled over the din.

Swede had no trouble making his booming voice heard above the noise of the crowd. "You guys talking about me again? Lily, these are the scruffy bunch of guys and extremely lovely ladies I've been telling you about." After reciting his friends' names, Swede said, "This is my friend Lily Sorenson. She's one of the new song-girls this year."

"Leave it to Swede to pick out the youngest and the best," Hazel Martz said.

"What? I'm sorry I couldn't hear you over the crowd noise," Swede yelled.

Yale repeated his wife's words in a much louder voice.

"Hey, you guys have cornered the best-looking ladies in town. I have to bring the prettiest girl in school just to keep up."

Otto shouted, "You poor baby; it must be a real strain. Have you told Lily you used to date Betsy Ross?"

Swede looked at his younger date and vigorously shook his head.

The young ladies put their heads close together so they could hear each other talk while the men began their usual loud play-by-play review of the game.

A young, blond waitress with a tray full of drinks balanced on one hand asked, "How many beers, and how many ginger ales here?"

Lily ordered ginger ale, and the rest raised one finger signifying they wanted a beer. The only two beverages served at the "Gag and Barf" during post game celebrations were each a nickel, so it was easy for the waitress to keep track of the tab.

Chapter 45

April 1928

Betty Johansson escorted Dr. Houser's last patient out the door and glanced at the clock on the wall. Four-forty; another twenty minutes and she would be off work. Not that she was all that anxious to leave. The young dental assistant felt fortunate to be working at Dr. Houser's dental office. He paid her an unheard of 35 dollars a week, and her job allowed her to meet some incredible people. Her boss's fame had earned him the privilege of working on the smiles of some of Hollywood's brightest stars as well as other prominent people around town. Only today, Jack Dempsey had brought his wife, Estelle, into the office and Betty had been able to chat with him while Dr. Houser was attending to the champ's wife. Yesterday, she had visited with movie idol, Buster Crabb, while he was waiting to have his famous smile fine-tuned.

"You can go home now, Betty," Bud called from his office.

"That's alright. I still have some paperwork to do before I leave."

Bud's wide grin lit up his deeply-tanned face as he walked out of his office carrying his coat and tie over his arm. "Actually, I have to get out of here if I'm going to get in some practice time before dark. The Olympic Games are only three months from now, and I'm still badly out of shape."

Betty sighed as she looked at Bud's trim waist and arms almost bulging out of his sleeves. She thought, "If that is what you call out of shape, please Lord send me someone that's this out of shape."

"You'll lock up before you leave?" He called as he went out the door.

"Of course, Doctor."

*   *   *

Between 5:00 and 5:30 each evening, members of the USC varsity football team practicing for the 1928 fall season watched a familiar figure walk across Bovard Field to the discus ring. Some preferred watching the all-time Trojan great carrying the discus. Other eyes were glued to the beautiful brunette in a skirt and sweater walking alongside him.

"Shouldn't you be starting to shop for clothes to wear in Amsterdam?" Bud asked.

"Are you trying to get rid of me?" Dawn replied.

"Of course not; I just thought you might be getting tired of watching me do the same old thing every night."

"I never get tired of being with you, honey, but I sometimes wonder why you're working so hard. You're throwing the discus almost 10 feet farther than your winning toss at Paris."

"Your dad once advised me that if I want to make sure of winning my event, my worst toss had to be better than my opponent's best."

"I still miss him so much."

"Of course you do, and so do I. Do you want to take your mother with us to the Olympics?"

"She doesn't enjoy travel that much. Her women's group at church and her bridge club keeps her busy."

Bud squatted into his usual crouch, made a fast spinning-move and arched the discus high in the air toward white chalk lines drawn across the grass. "Can you see how far that went?" he asked.

It looks like it's just short of the 150 foot mark."

"I have to do better than that."

"Oh, gee. Only 149 feet in your street clothes and leather soled shoes on your first toss. What will we do?"

He laughed. "You won't think it's so funny when some giant from Finland pounds me into the ground. No one knows how far those apes are slinging the saucer." He ran and retrieved the discus, and then asked. "What are we having for dinner tonight?"

"See if you can remember."

"Is today Tuesday?"

"No, it's Wednesday."

Hmm, let's see. Did you say you were fixing meat loaf?"

He crouched again, spun, and sent his next toss a few feet past his first mark.

"That one went a little over 150," she said.

"Okay, I give up. I forgot what you told me."

"You are impossible. We're meeting our Friendship Bible Class at the church and leading them over to our house for a potluck."

"Of course I remembered. I was just teasing you."

"Yeah, sure you were. Why don't I go meet them? That will give you a little more time to practice, shower, and change your clothes."

He leaned over and kissed her lightly on the lips. "That's very sweet of you. I'll be ready by the time you get home."

A couple of football players watched the attractive woman walk off the field and climb into her Packard Twin-Six."

"How does he get home?" one youngster asked.

"They have two cars."

"I never heard of one family having two cars. They must be rich."

"I don't know about that. I heard she got hers free and he only paid 200 dollars for a brand new 1928 Gardner Cabriolet."

"How did they do that?"

"Her parents gave her the Packard when she graduated from high school, and Gardner Motor Company sold Bud his car for less than half-price just for riding around the coliseum on the hood a few times and telling people how much he liked their new car."

"Whooof. That's less than the cost of a model T Ford. I was there when he stood up on the hood and rode around the track, but I didn't know they were going to give him that kind of deal just for endorsing their product."

"I guess being a successful athlete has some advantages."

They both watched as the gorgeous brunette's hair blew back as she accelerated her automobile down the street.

"More than one advantage if you ask me," the other player observed.

Chapter 46

July 1928

The 1924 Dodge taxi pulled up near the boarding ramp leading to the U.S. America, and Bud and Dawn got their first look at the ship that they would be cruising on for the next several days. As they climbed out of the taxi, they could see the huge white letters that had been painted across the length of the ship reading "UNITED STATES OLYMPIC TEAM." Healthy looking young men and women were pulling black suitcases out of autos and bidding farewell to friends and relatives.

As the taxi driver pulled their luggage out of the trunk, Bud asked, "Aren't you excited, honey?"

"I'm happy, but kind of sad too. The last time we boarded a ship for Europe, Martha was with us and so many of our friends were already on board. It doesn't seem right going without all of them."

"I know; I feel the same way. Leighton and Eleanor will be with us, and Johnny Weissmuller will be making the trip. I guess we'll just have to make some new friends."

"I like the friends we have." She slipped her arm around his waist and shot him a playful glance. "At least we'll be sleeping together this time."

"Yes, and that's very important to me."

A long, black car with small American flags on each front fender pulled between them and the boarding ramp. The impressive looking automobile was escorted by two black cars in front and two others in back. Men jumped out of the smaller cars and formed a double line leading from the bigger automobile to the ramp. With his always present braided cap, sun glasses and corncob pipe, General Douglas MacArthur was probably the most easily recognized man in the United States.

"It looks like the General has arrived," Bud said.

"Wow, I knew MacArthur was our Olympic chairman this year, but it never occurred to me he might be sailing with us."

"I didn't know it either," Bud said.

"Isn't that Leighton and Eleanor up on the deck waving to us?"

Bud and Dawn waved toward their friends and pointed to the General's car indicating they might take a while longer boarding.

*   *   *

After several days aboard the steamship America, Bud and Dawn were anxious to arrive in Cherbourg. The cruise to Europe had been pleasurable, but not as exhilarating as their cruise to France in 1924. The excitement of the young ladies on the first United States Women's Track and Field Team had been fun to watch and the meals had been as good as ever. However, ghosts of their friends and Bud's former teammates seemed to roam the decks reminding them of all the thrills of that first voyage where they were not only representing their country, but also their school. It was great spending evenings dancing close and then going to their stateroom, but the intrigue that had existed about whether Bud and Dawn would be married during the Paris Olympics was all but forgotten.

Things were just different two years after Bud had received his degree from dental school and Dawn had last attended art classes and graduated from USC. This year Bud and his friend Leighton Dye would be competing with the Los Angeles Athletic Club instead of the Southern California Trojans. In contrast to 1924, Bud was now the heavy favorite to win another gold medal in the only event he was entering, the discus. The friendship of Leighton Dye and his wife, Eleanor, had kept the cruise pleasant for the first few days, but now all were anxious to reach their destination. The Captain had estimated they would arrive in Holland in another couple of days.

The night before they were to dock in Cherbourg, Bud and Dawn were strolling along the deck and making plans for their second honeymoon travels after the Olympic Games had ended. Of course, they both wanted to see Holland, but she wasn't sure about the track meet that was scheduled for Germany just a week after the closing ceremonies. Both agreed a trip back to Paris was definitely a must.

They stopped talking when they noticed a man in a military uniform who seemed to be heading right toward them.

"Good morning, Dr. Houser and Mrs. Houser. I'm Lieutenant Carver, aide to General Douglas MacArthur. The General has asked me to extend an invitation for you to join him for dinner in his cabin at 7:00 this evening."

Bud and Dawn were speechless for a few seconds. No one had even seen the General since he had boarded the ship in New York, and now they were being extended a private dinner invitation.

"Of course," Bud stammered. "It will be an honor to have dinner with the General."

As the young lieutenant walked away, Dawn was almost dancing with pleasure. "General Douglas MacArthur asked us to have dinner with him. He's more popular than Calvin Coolidge, and he wants to spend the evening with us. What should I wear?"

"Your white, knit dress with the black trim and your matching white hat always looks nice. You can't hardly run out to a department store and buy a new outfit."

Chapter 47

Lieutenant Carver greeted them at the door with, "Good evening, Dr. and Mrs. Houser. May I present General Douglas MacArthur."

The General came over and shook each of their hands. He looked completely different without his trademark cap and aviator sunglasses. His thinning hair and warm, friendly smile was much less imposing than the persona he presented to the public. He waved them to a couch and sat in a chair facing them.

Bud and Dawn glanced around at a stateroom at least three times the size of their own and much more luxurious. A table had already been set with fine china, ornate silver, a white linen tablecloth and white linen napkins.

"Thank you for inviting us to dinner," Bud began.

"It's my pleasure. I've been following your career ever since you beat Pat McDonald in the shot put when you were in high school."

"And I've been reading about you ever since you led the Rainbow Division through France during the war."

"You are not at all like I expected," Dawn said.

MacArthur chuckled. "If you heard I'm aloof and egotistical, you heard right. However, I'm only that way with people who believe peace comes free. I've heard you grew up in a small town, Dr. Houser."

"Please, just call me 'Bud.' Yes, I lived on a farm in Winigan, Missouri. Then, when my father died, I moved to Oxnard to live with my sister."

"I grew up at Fort Selden, New Mexico. It was hardly a town. My first memory was the sound of bugles. I learned to ride and shoot before I could read or write."

"I delayed reading and writing a bit myself. I didn't start formal schooling until I was twelve," Bud said.

"Would you two like something to drink?"

"Either ice tea or lemonade would be nice," Dawn replied.

"How about a mixture of the two?"

"We've never tried that but it sounds good," Bud said.

The General nodded to his aide, and then added, "Bring me the usual."

The aide walked to a small bar against one wall, poured the two soft drinks over ice, poured a glass of amber liquid from a black-labeled bottle, and handed each one their drink.

Bud took a sip of his drink and then said, "It isn't often a person gets to talk to someone like you. Do you mind if I ask you a few questions?"

"Of course not."

"Our local newspapers publish editorials that say the World War was the war to end all wars. Dawn and I read the Bible and have studied history, and it seems to us there have always been wars. We have wondered if what we are reading in the papers is too optimistic. What is your opinion?"

"You two are quite astute. Let me warn you, this kind of question can often produce a rather lengthy sermon."

"It would be our honor to hear what you have to say," Dawn said.

"You also read in the newspaper about people robbing banks and gas stations and killing people for money. I'm sure that's not easy for decent people like you to comprehend. Many people don't realize that in some parts of the world, whole countries are run by the same kind of thieves and murderers. Whereas robbers might kill one or two innocent people, brutal dictators think nothing about killing tens of thousands. It's difficult for people in our free society to realize how much of the world is controlled by evil men. Maybe someday that will change, but I doubt if it will happen in my lifetime or even yours. I've been a soldier all my life, so I leave it up to politicians to debate the controversial issues which divide men's minds. Like all soldiers, I pray for peace, for we're the ones who bear the deepest wounds and scars of war. Always in my ears ring the ominous words of Plato, 'Only the dead have seen the end of war.'"

Bud and Dawn sat wide-eyed; awed by the wisdom of this great man.

The General grinned. "I didn't invite you here to frighten you. Hopefully our country will remain at peace for many years to come. The reason I brought you here, Bud, is because I would like to have you to carry our flag and lead our Olympic team in the opening Parade of Nations."

"Wow, that's quite an honor. I carried the flag in the closing ceremonies four years ago after I had won two gold medals. How do you know I'll win anything this year?"

"It's not about what you might or might not win. It is about the way you've conducted your life and the example you have set for young men around our country. I know you could have been a star athlete in several sports, but you worked hard and earned your dental degree. And now you are taking time off from your practice to once again represent your country in the largest athletic event in the world."

Dawn glanced over at her husband's moist eyes. She had always marveled how such a powerful man could be so sensitive.

"It would be my honor, General."

MacArthur's aide answered a knock on the door, and a ship's steward wheeled in a cart filled with several covered silver platters. No one needed to tell Bud and Dawn that a delicious meal awaited them. The aroma gave it away.

Once dinner was over, Bud and Dawn progressed from their early evening nervousness to comfortable conversation with the great man.

General MacArthur leaned back in his chair. "I'm sure you've been asked this hundreds of times, Bud, but how does a guy your size whip all those giants you compete against?"

Bud flashed the general a grin. "What giants?"

Chapter 48

Bud sprawled on the bed of their hotel room in Amsterdam and watched his wife as she got dressed. In his white suit, white shirt, and red, white, and blue striped tie, he was already clothed for the Opening Ceremony of the IX Olympiad. His white hat, with the hatband matching his tie, sat on the bed next to him.

She smiled at him. "Is there some fascination you have with the way I get dressed, Dr. Houser?"

"I prefer watching you take your clothes off, but the efficient way you get ready to go out impresses me."

"I guess that's as good an excuse as any."

"No… really. Look at the way I get dressed. First I put on my pants, button up the fly, put on my belt and buckle it, and then I put on my shirt. This requires that I unbuckle my belt, unbutton my fly, spread my legs apart so my pants won't fall down, and then tuck in my shirttail. Then I have to button up…"

"Stop…" she giggled. I'll never be ready if you start me laughing. That wouldn't be so funny if it wasn't true."

"What can I say? I'm just a guy."

"Do you think that Queen Wilhelmine will be in the grandstands when you carry our flag by the royal box?"

"Not after she said she considers the games a 'demonstration of paganism.' I've heard that Prince Hendrick will announce the official opening."

"Why did Pope Pius object to women participating in track and field? They wear at least as much clothes as the swimmers and divers."

Bud shrugged.

Dawn looked in the mirror and gave her cheeks one last pat with her powder puff. "With over 2800 athletes, the parade of nations could take a while. Do you know when the American team will be marching around the track?"

"All I know is the Greek team will be first, and the host Dutch team is last."

"With all of the band music and the people from different nations, it's still exciting no matter how long it takes. It will be nice watching the first women to ever compete on the United States track team march around the stadium."

"It will indeed."

*   *   *

Accustomed to barking orders amid the crack of gunfire and exploding artillery shells, General MacArthur had no problem being heard above the marching coordinator who held up his megaphone and called out the time for each country's team to enter the stadium. The crisp evening air contrasted the 113 degree heat wave in Paris four years ago. A light drizzle had fallen the last few days. Although stars shone brightly in the clear black sky, the ground remained damp and moisture still breathed its chilly breath on the waiting the athletes.

Along with athletes from 46 countries, the 400 plus Team USA had watched the first-ever Olympic flame being lit, listened to a medley of national anthems by an accomplished Dutch band, and heard Prince Hendrick of Mecklenburg give the opening speech in a language known to none.

After sending team after team out onto the track, the coordinator barked, "The United Kingdom will be next, followed by the United States." He pointed to the British team, held up one finger, and then pointed to Team USA and held up two, signifying they would follow.

200

MacArthur had already lined up the men eight abreast, with Bud by himself in the front, and gave these last-minute instructions. "We are here to represent the greatest country on earth. We did not come here to lose gracefully. We came here to win decisively. Stand up straight; hold your heads erect, and keep our flag flying high in the air." He watched for the coordinators signal, and then said, "This is your time, ladies and gentlemen of the United States Olympic Team."

The roar from the spectators at the area of the stadium where the Americans were congregated brought smiles and waves from the marching youngsters representing their country in this, the biggest international event of their lives.

Bud held the Stars and Stripes high as they marched from the entryway past the first part of the packed stadium and toward the royal box. As he glanced around the track, he saw something disturbing. Each nation's flag had an ugly brown stain at its lowest point. Looking to the team now passing the royal box, he saw the reason. Out of deference to the royal family and their distinguished guests, the flag bearer lowered his nation's flag as he passed. With only a few feet separating the bottom point of their flag from the ground, this caused it to drag across the muddy turf for a few feet before the flag bearer again raised it to, once again, wave in the gentle wind.

Should he follow protocol and avoid additional criticism from some who already resented American domination in so many sports? There was no doubt that was what he was expected to do.

As the American team drew closer to the center of the stadium, he made his decision. Marching past the royal box, he grabbed the flagpole firmly in one hand, kept it flying high, and with the other hand, took off his hat and bowed his head toward the watching dignitaries. Apparently, flags dragging on the ground had not pleased people from other nations either, because the crowd leaped to their feet and cheered. Glancing toward the royal box, he was relieved to see that those seated there were also standing and applauding.

"Good decision," he heard from a girl's voice to the side and behind him. Turning, he saw a pretty teenager grinning at him. Betty Robinson, the teenage phenom Americans hoped would win a medal in the women's 100 meter dash, agreed with him, and she was not afraid to express her feelings amidst all of the older men surrounding her.

As the American team walked past the stands on the far side of the stadium, Bud glanced across the field and saw that no flag following the American flag contained a stain. The team now marching past the royal box held their flag high in the air as well. Whether or not he won a medal in the discus in a few days, he felt like he had already contributed something worthwhile to the Games.

Chapter 49

Dawn opened her eyes and looked out the hotel window at the clear blue sky that was Northern Holland. Their first honeymoon had been incredibly romantic; boating on the lake, sunbathing, hiking through the woods, and spending evenings wandering through Lake Arrowhead Village or just toasting their toes by the fireplace of their cabin and inhaling the delicious aroma of pine logs burning. It was a pleasant way for a newly married couple to spend their first days and nights together. However, now that they had been married for four years the excitement of being in a foreign land, and seeing things they might never see again was a once-in-a-lifetime opportunity. She propped up on one elbow and looked down at her sleeping husband, remembering how her heart had beat faster the first time she had seen his sculpted and tanned body in those brief little track shorts and his sleeveless track shirt. "And now you are all mine," she said pulling a long sun-bleached hair out of his chest.

"Ouch. What a way to wake a guy up," he complained. Then seeing the grin on her face, Bud quickly added. "I've had plenty of sleep anyway."

*   *   *

Neither Bud nor Dawn had expected the city of water to be such a fascinating place. Downtown Amsterdam was a maze of canals with more bridges than anyone could count; more even than Paris. At night the bridges were romantically illuminated. Each day they found interesting places to stroll. Near their hotel was the old and picturesque Majer Bridge.

With hundreds of lights covering its fairly large expanse, it soon became their favorite spot.

The concierge at the hotel had told them, "'Majer' is Dutch for skinny."

"But it is not skinny; it's wide," Dawn had remarked.

"It was skinny when they originally built and named it in 1620. When they rebuilt it in 1871, it kept its original name."

As they had experienced four years ago in Paris, the span of time between the opening ceremony and Bud's event left more than enough time to see the city as well as take in selected Olympic events. They visited the Raepenhofje on the Palmgracht, a gatehouse built sideways with a small, round gate and a beautiful commemorative stone which said, "This hofjie was founded and built by Pieter Adriaensz in 1648." On further inquiry, they discovered the hofjies originated in the 14th century and were built and funded by wealthy citizens for the old and needy.

Just off of Amsterdam's main street, Bud and Dawn discovered a secluded court of houses with a quiet courtyard and garden. From an old wooden bench they gazed across a breathtaking flower garden to what looked like medieval wooden houses.

"If those houses could talk, I'll bet they would have quite a story to tell," Dawn said.

Words spoken in halting, but understandable, English came from behind the couple. "Five hundred and fifty years of stories. I've often wished I could hear the tales they would tell."

Bud and Dawn turned to see a white-haired, old man trimming some tulips.

"You two see the third house down? It is the oldest original one. It was built in 1475. All the others have been renovated more recently."

"What you mean by more recently?" Bud asked.

"During the 17th and 18th centuries."

Bud and Dawn looked at each other and smiled.

*   *   *

As the days passed, Bud and dawn fell into a comfortable routine. She would join him at an area outside of the Olympic stadium for his morning practice session, and then they would either spend the afternoon sightseeing or watching gymnastics, equestrian, rowing, or other Olympic events. During that time, the spirit of the Games was best exemplified by Australian rower, Henry Pearce. Midway through his quarterfinal race, he stopped rowing to allow a family of ducks to pass single file in front of his boat. Pearce won the race anyway, and later won the gold medal.

On the days when they chose sightseeing, art galleries provided them with glimpses of 18th and 19th century art, and coffee houses provided a relaxing diversion. Dawn's favorite afternoon was spent at the Singel, the oldest floating flower garden in Amsterdam, where unique flowers were displayed on floating barges. She sniffed Dutch tulips and geraniums, while he was more fascinated by the miniature cypresses. Bud enjoyed the day at the floating gardens, although she accused him of being more interested in lunch at a quaint, old coffee house nearby.

By far Bud's favorite day was the one they spent sailing in a rather large boat on the Zuyderzee. Accustomed to Southern California weather, it was unusual for them to bundle up for a boat ride.

*   *   *

Bud would be hard pressed to tell what he had eaten for dinner at café 'Het Tolhuis', at 7 Buiksloterweg, but whatever it was, it had been totally satisfying. Downtown Amsterdam was compact enough for them to walk from their hotel room to the restaurant, leaving plenty of time to enjoy the lights on the Majer Bridge.

As the couple strolled hand in hand, he said, "Thinking back on your childhood, what is the first thing you can remember?"

"Let's see. I don't know which came first, but I remember standing on the seat and trying to turn the huge steering wheel of Dad's car in the driveway of our house on Pico Boulevard. I remember Dad picking me up and carrying me out into the ocean on one of his shoulders. I miss him so much."

"Of course you do; he was such a great guy."

"What is your earliest memory?"

"Standing by the cross where they had buried my mother and wondering why God didn't like me."

"You didn't have a very happy childhood, did you?"

"My sisters and brothers gave me more than my share of love, but times were tough. I was working in the fields by the time I was seven years old."

"I know. Maybe that's why you're so strong, and why you won't let anyone beat you."

He laughed. "I hope you can still say that after the Games are over."

"I will."

They walked in silence for quite a distance before he said, "I want our kids to grow up with memories like yours, not like mine."

"I know you do. During every Trojan football game, I knew how badly you wanted to be out there with your friends, but you stuck it out in dental school so that you could provide a better life for us."

"Did you ever think about how much your father influenced me to do that?"

"I thought it was Jim Thorpe."

"How do you think Jim Thorpe knew about the decisions I was wrestling with, or even where he could find me that day?"

She stopped and grabbed his arm, "No... You think Dad put him up to that?"

"The more I think about it, the more convinced I am that's exactly what happened. But that wasn't the only way your Dad swayed my decision. He was so subtle; he could convince me of something without even letting me know that he was doing it."

"Dad was good at that, but his subtlety was always for the other person's benefit. I don't know how many times he made me think his ideas originated with me. I would tell him how I felt about something, and he would smile and agree with me. Later I would remember that he was the one who had planted that idea into my head."

As they neared the Majer Bridge he said, "Is it my imagination, or do those lights on the water get prettier every night."

Chapter 50

Bud held a black umbrella over Dawn's head, and wrapped his arm tightly around her to keep her warm. It was near the end of the first day of the track-and-field competition, and both of them were shocked at their team's poor performance. Up until today, the sun's irregular appearances, amid intermittent rain, had not seemed to affect the members of the United States Olympic Team. Not too many days ago, American men had won three gold medals in the swimming events, with Johnny Weissmuller winning the 100 meter race, George Kojac taking the 100 meter backstroke, and Team USA prevailing in the 4 X 200 freestyle relay. Then, Peter Desjardis added two more gold medals, one in the platform diving, and the other in the springboard event. The women kept up with their male counterparts again when Martha Norelius and Albina Ospowich each won gold medals in swimming. Ladies from the USA team won another gold medal in the relay. To further add to the medal count, Helen Meany won the springboard diving and Elizabeth Becker took the gold medal in the platform dive. One more gold medal in rowing and another in wrestling, and several silver and bronze medals in various events had made it look like Team USA would again dominate the Games.

The highlight of the Olympics every four years was the track-and-field events, and there had been no reason to suspect the Americans would win any fewer contests than they had in 1924. Today the sky had opened up and poured rain on the Olympians and the spectators. Athletes from the United States had not performed well in the mud. The day had begun with Percy Williams from Canada shocking the world by beating Charley Paddock and a host of other sprinters in both the 100-meter and 200-meter races. Even stranger, Great Britain and Germany took the silver and bronze with no American finishing better than fourth in either event. Ray Barbuti gave the wet, shivering Americans something to cheer about when he won the gold medal in the 400 meter race, but again Germany and Great Britain took the silver and bronze. With their star athlete from 1924, Paavo Nurmi, performing his usual magic by collecting three gold medals, Finland dominated the distance runs again winning the 1500-, 5000-, and 10,000-meter runs. Americans were not expected to win any medals in these distance races, and they performed as poorly as was expected. Then, Great Britain won the 800 meter, and France won the marathon with no Americans placing in either event.

Bud and Dawn walked out of the stadium with the sickening realization that our supposedly powerful United States track team had tied China with only one medal on the first day of the track-and-field competition.

"Do you think our guys couldn't handle the weather?" Dawn asked.

"Well, we do have a lot of athletes from Southern California where we don't see much rain, but you have to give these other men credit. Percy Williams ran the 100 meters in 10.8 and the 200 in 20.8 in the rain and mud, and the Germans and English were only a tenth of a second back. Those times are pretty hard to beat in any conditions."

"So these other countries have improved more than we knew. Do you think your competition in the discus will be that much tougher too?"

"I know it will. I've been watching these guys from Finland throwing the saucer out close to 160."

"And you've already thrown it 160 a few days ago in practice."

"Yes, I did, but it wasn't raining. I've heard that this storm will last for several more days."

She took his arm and looked up at him. "You know how I know you will win? Because you always do your best when things get the toughest."

"How do you know that?"

"I read it in the newspaper."

*   *   *

Loyal Americans ignored their team's poor performance on the first day of the track- and-field competition and braved the rain and cold once again to cheer on their athletes.

Bud had spent close to an hour practicing the discus in a pouring rain. He wanted to be at his best in what he felt would be the last time he would be competing in the sport that had brought him so much pleasure over the years. He and Dawn walked into the stadium just before the 110-meter hurdles race began. Sid Atkinson of South Africa won the race, but Steven Anderson and John Collier of the USA took the silver and bronze. In just the first race, members of Team USA had won more medals than they had the day before. David Burley of Great Britain won the 400 meter hurdles, but again, Americans Frank Cuhel and F. Morgan Taylor took the silver and bronze. Toivo Loukola upset teammate Paavo Nurmi in the steeplechase with Finland again sweeping away all three medals. The American fans began getting restless.

Some of the same men who had not been able to win any medals yesterday were getting ready to run the 4X 100-meter relay. People wondered if they would be able to accomplish as a team what they had not been able to do individually. Frank Wykoff took off like a demon on the first leg of the relay, leaving other counties' sprinters with nothing to look at but the youngster's back. The baton was passed perfectly, and Jimmy Quinn refused to surrender any of the lead as he dashed around the track toward a waiting Charley Borah. On the third leg of the race, Borah was almost at full speed when Quinn passed the baton, and he ran like he was on fast, dry ground instead of the wet sloppy track his feet were sloshing through. He rounded the last turn and looked ahead to Hank Russell. One more successful exchange on the last leg of the relay, and the Americans would have their first gold medal, but the baton was soaking wet. Bud and Dawn and all those around them were holding their breath when Borah attempted to pass the baton to his waiting teammate. The baton touched Russell's wrist just above his hand, and the crowd gasped. The American who had been chosen to run the last leg of the relay reached back and gripped the baton, but the exchange had lost the Americans some time. Russell raced through the mud around the final turn trying with every ounce of strength he possessed to widen the distance between him and the man behind him. He sprinted toward the finish line not daring to glance back at the German anchor man quickly closing the gap.

Dawn jumped up and down, screamed, and pounded her fist against Bud's arm as Hank Russell raced across the finish line two-tenths of a second ahead of the last German sprinter. "Wow, wow, wow," she squealed.

"No more complaining about my body language at Trojan football games," Bud said.

"The next time we watch a 4 by 100-meter relay, I'm going to have a bodyguard with me."

The 4 X 400-meter relay didn't require quite the precision of the 4 x 100, but the finish was almost as close. The American team of George Baird, Bud Spencer, Fred Alderman and Ray Barbuti finished just six-tenths of a second ahead of the now frustrated Germans.

Bob King elevated American spirit with a leap of 6-4 ½ to edge out team member Benjamin Hedges as they produced a gold and silver in the high jump. Then Team USA finished the day on a high note with Sabin Carr, William Droegemueller, and Charles McGinnis sweeping all three medals in the pole vault.

Holding the umbrella above his wife's head and walking alongside her toward the exit, Bud asked, "Was that enough excitement for today?"

"Whoof. That was really fun. Our men really came through. I hope the rain lets up before the day of your event though."

Chapter 51

This was the moment that sports-minded women around the world had waited for. Loud cheers erupted from various places in the grandstands as athletes from different countries ran onto the field to begin their warm-ups. Members of the first-ever women's Olympic track team smiled and waved to fans who had come from faraway places to watch them perform. They would only be competing in five events, but it was a start. In their wisdom, the Olympic committee had scheduled the women's events close to the end of the competition, but saved the men's long jump, triple jump, shot put, and discus for the finale. No one complained about the ladies' unremarkable position in the order of events. They were here to bring home the first medals ever won by women in the 100- meter dash, the 800 meter run, the 4 X 100 meter relay, the high jump, and the discus. The storms that had plagued the men's team had been courteous enough to move farther south and provide a pleasant, though crisp, day for the ladies.

As Bud and Dawn found their seat in the grandstands, she said, "Now I know how you felt when you wanted to be out on the football field and baseball diamond while the Trojans were playing."

"Maybe you should try out for the 1932 Olympics."

"I'm afraid that ship has sailed. I'll be 30 years old by then."

*   *   *

By the time the high jump bar was set at 5 feet, only three women remained in the competition. Americans cheered when Mildred Wiley cleared 5 feet to match the jumps of Carolyn Gisolf of the Netherlands and Ethel Catherwood of Canada.

"Do you think you could jump that high?" Bud asked.

"Nope."

"How do you know?"

"I tried it one time with my girlfriends at LA High."

"How high did you jump?"

"More than any of them, but my best was only four feet even."

"You cleared four feet when you were in high school? Didn't anyone tell you that you get better with practice?"

"We didn't have a track team, and I was only interested in softball and basketball."

"Because you were good at those sports?"

"I guess. Who knew that someday I would be sitting in Holland watching women jump over bamboo poles?"

"Maybe someday they will have women's softball and basketball in the Olympics."

"Probably, when I'm about 80."

Ethel Catherwood cleared the bar at 5 feet 1 ¼ inches. Carolyn Gisolf followed, and Mildred Wiley also cleared the bar. With the bar set at 5 foot 2 ½ inches, all three women missed on the first two attempts. On her third attempt, Ethel Catherwood barely cleared the bar, bringing an enormous cheer from the Canadian fans. Carolyn Gisolf missed on her final attempt leaving Mildred Wiley with one jump left to stay in contention for the gold. She sprinted across the grass, leaped high in the air, and barely nicked the bar on the way down. Americans held their breath as the bar wobbled up and down and then fell into the sawdust pit.

"Oh, gee! I thought she'd made it," Dawn exclaimed.

"She tied for second. That's not too bad."

Next, Lina Radke of Germany finished ahead of Kinue Hitomi of Japan and Inga Gentzell of Sweden in the 800 meter, with the American women straggling far behind.

"Why aren't we any good in the distance races?" Dawn asked.

Bud shrugged. "Maybe it's not that we're so bad as much as other countries are better."

"I still wonder why," Dawn said.

Women's Team USA finished second in the 4 X 100-meter relay, and while they were running, Lillian Copeland gave their team its third silver medal by taking second in the discus behind Halina Konopacka of Poland.

"That was great," Bud remarked.

"Are you talking about the relay or the discus?" Dawn asked.

"They were both good performances, but did you see the size of those ladies from Sweden and Denmark that Lillian had to compete against?"

"You should see how you look next to those monsters in the men's weight events."

"They're not that much bigger than me."

"Oh, yeah? Come up here and look at yourself some-time."

"Good idea. I might do that. Speaking of size difference, look at Betty Robinson warming up with the other sprinters."

"Oh, my. She looks like a little girl next to all those powerful looking sprinters. Do you think she has any chance?"

"Probably not, but it's quite an honor for a high school girl to even make the team. Do you want something to drink while we're waiting for the final race?"

Bud and Dawn sipped their coffee and watched the crowd of women athletes gathering to see who would claim the title of the fastest woman in the world.

"Isn't it funny how we change our habits when we're in a foreign country?" Bud remarked.

"That's right. We wouldn't even think about drinking coffee in the Coliseum. Of course, the weather is seldom this cold."

"And they don't brew coffee that tastes this good in Los Angeles."

When the sprinters took off, Betty Robinson was about in the middle of the pack with several runners ahead of her. At the halfway mark, she pulled into third place and looked like she might take home a medal after all. As they neared the finish line, she pulled even with Fanny Rosenfeld and Ethel Smith, both of Canada.

Dawn was cheering and pushing so hard against Bud he could hardly stay in his seat as the three women crossed the finish line. "Did she win? Did she win?" she screamed.

"It looked to me like she did, but it was so close. We better wait until they make the official announcement."

A tremendous roar came from the American section of the stadium when it was officially announced that this pretty American teenager had indeed captured the gold medal. The scoreboard showed Betty's time at 12.2 seconds with the two Canadians one- tenth of a second behind at 12.3 seconds.

Betty Robinson grinned and waved toward the crowd as she walked toward the grass just off the track. A man holding a large camera with International Newsreel written across it recorded this moment.

"I want to see that picture," Bud said.

"That shouldn't be too hard. It will be on the front page of every newspaper in America," Dawn exclaimed.

"Maybe most newspapers in the world."

Chapter 52

Bud stared down at a stack of hotcakes that had been prepared in a way cooks in the U.S. could only hope to duplicate. He poured more than enough hot syrup across the top, took a small bite, leaned back, and sipped his coffee. He stared at the rain splashing against the dining room window and beyond it to the water rushing past the curb in front of their hotel.

"Lost your appetite?" Dawn asked. "I don't see that too often."

"Apparently being the favorite adds more pressure than when no one expects me to win."

"Does this weather worry you?"

"I wish it could have been as nice as yesterday, but I'm glad our ladies' team got a break."

"You're going to win again. You're throwing the discus farther than anyone in the country. Ten feet farther than your winning toss in Paris."

Have you seen this new kid, James Corson?"

"I've never heard of him. Is he on our team?"

"He is. I watched him throw the discus about 158 feet in practice the other day."

"How about the Finnish team you were telling me about?"

"No one knows how far they're slinging the platter. They keep their distances under wraps up until the Games. You can be sure they want to avenge their loss in Paris."

"I wonder what Glenn Hartcranft and Thomas Lieb are doing these days. I miss them a lot," Dawn commented.

"I guess we're getting on in years when we look back on the good old days. Those guys probably had the good sense to put the field events behind them by now."

"Yes, but you're a little younger. You hadn't reached your full potential in 1924."

"Where do you come up with all these ideas?"

"I read the paper just like everyone else."

"Who do the writers predict will win today?"

"If you didn't already know the answer to that question, you would be having the waitress bring you another stack of hotcakes by now."

*　　　*　　　*

Shortly before the field events began, the rain let up long enough for Ed Hamm of Team USA to win the long jump with a leap of 25 feet 4 ½ inches. Silvio Cator of Haiti took second just five inches short of Hamm, and another American, Alfred Bates took third with a jump of 24 feet and 3 ¼ inches."

As Bud and James Corson warmed up, they listened to the announcer give the results of each event. After the finals of the long jump, they heard American John Doherty announced as the bronze medal winner of the decathlon, and another teammate, Levi Casey, pronounced winner of a silver medal in the triple jump.

Concluding their warm-up, Bud kidded, "It certainly is a comfort to know that our team has already won the majority of medals before we even start the weight events."

Not being familiar with Bud's dead-pan style of humor, Corson answered. "You know, Dr. Houser, I've never won an Olympic medal. I'm scared half out of my mind. Even my home town newspaper predicted me to take fourth or fifth place."

"If you can beat that fear, you will win a medal today," Bud assured him.

"You really think so?"

"It's not what I think that counts, it's what you think. If you think you're going to win a medal, you will. If you're afraid you're going to lose, then that is what will happen."

"It's as simple as that?"

Bud grinned. "Not really. You have to have the talent too. Some of the guys we compete against are going to be mighty shaky when they step into the ring. Their knees will get weak, and their stomachs will be queasy. They'll even be short of breath. I have seen it happen over and over. As a result, they won't be able to get off their best tosses. Believe me, James, I saw you throw that discus far enough when we were practicing to win. All you have to do now is step up to the plate, think tough, and do what you have the ability to do."

"Wow! I think I feel better all already."

"You know, the only reason I'm telling you this is because this will be my last Olympics."

The man in the broadcast booth announced that Sweden, Hungary, and Norway had finished one, two, and three in the javelin.

The huge athletes from Germany, Sweden, and France began the first round of discus competition, and, in the blinding rain, none even came close to 150 feet. Mercifully, the pouring rain let up, and the sun actually broke through the clouds as James Corson stepped up to the ring for his first toss. Bud could tell by the expression on his face that he had conquered his fear and replaced it with a fierce determination. He felt proud as the young athlete crouched low facing away from his target in the same manner he had pioneered while still at Oxnard High school. It was like he was watching himself as the young man uncoiled his body reaching maximum speed just as he launched the discus high and long. "What have I done?" Bud thought as he watched the platter sail well beyond the other distances. When he heard the distance of 154 feet 6 inches, he knew his lecture had been well received, but had he lost his own opportunity for a gold medal in the process? James Corson's distance held up throughout the first round until it was finally time for Bud's first toss.

As he walked toward the discus ring, he glanced up into the gray sky. It had started to drizzle again, but Bud had thrown the discus in worse conditions. In spite of James' flag planted almost 155 feet across the grass, he felt the same confidence that had propelled him to victory so many times in the past. His task was obvious: throw the platter past the last marker, and that's what he intended to do. The grass and dirt in the ring had turned a little muddy, but he hadn't noticed anyone else slipping, so he decided to ignore his footing and just concentrate on accelerating his spin just before his release. He went into his now-famous crouch. People had always looked at his size as a disadvantage. What he knew, that he had shared with only a few others, was that his smaller stature gave him more room to gain speed within the ring.

Putting all of his strength into the spin, he pushed up as hard as he could with the muscles in his legs, back, shoulders, and arms, and with a tremendous burst of energy released the discus. His toss careened out less than 100 feet across the wet grass. Bud was incredulous. He heard the loud groans coming from the American section of the grandstands and imagined Dawn with her face in her hands. Not in high school, not in college, not in meets for the Los Angeles Athletic Club - never, in any event in which he had participated had he experienced anything like this. Worst of all, he had no idea why this had happened. At the most crucial moment possible, the discus had slipped out of his hand.

The rain began to fall harder, making it unlikely for anyone to surpass James Corson's first throw. Bud watched each athlete perform, but in-between tried to recreate everything he had done that resulted in losing control of the discus. No answers came.

Somehow, during the second round of throws, a monster of a man, Antero Kivi of Finland, got off a toss that landed about even with James' flag. The official that placed the marker called out that it was 154 feet 11 inches, just five inches past the young American's toss.

Bud's mind traveled back to that sunny day in Pasadena and remembered the shocked expression on the face of Olympic Champion, Pat McDonald, when this high school kid named "Houser" had beaten him in the shot put. Was this his time to surrender his title to a young athlete?

Frank's second toss was a valiant effort in the rain, but landed a couple feet short of Kivi's flag.

It was time for Bud's second try. To the amazement of himself and everyone else in the crowd, the discus slipped from his hand once again and went only a few feet past his first embarrassing marker. As he trudged away from the discus ring, he felt angry, embarrassed, and completely frustrated. It was one thing to practice all those months, travel all the way to Amsterdam, and get beat. It was another thing to be completely humiliated. In spite of the cold and rain, he could feel his face burning and a cold sweat popping out under his arms.

To Bud, the final round felt somehow unreal. He watched each man step up to the ring, try to battle the elements and his own nerves, and then fail to reach the previous marks of Antero Kivi and James Corson. Finally it was time for the last man to make his last attempt. Bud stopped short of the discus ring and stared at the ground.

"What's he doing?" he heard a man's voice ask.

He recognized the second voice as James Corson. "I think he might be praying. That's what I would do if I was in his place."

Actually, Bud had only been staring at the ground trying to figure out what he was doing wrong. Unable to come up with any answers, he decided to do what Corson said he would do in these circumstances. "Okay, God. I know it's not fair to ask you to help me beat anyone. Just help me to do the best I know how to do. And by the way, I know you like me now."

He stepped into the discus ring for what he believed would be the very last time and went into his usual crouch facing away from all the distance markers. The rain was falling steady now. He didn't think about holding onto the discus or even about giving this toss his supreme effort, but as soon as the discus left his hand, he knew he would not walk away from this day's competition embarrassed. The rain fell onto Bud's bowed head and neck as he listened to the announcements on the loudspeaker.

"I now have the final standings in the shot put, hammer throw, and discus. Johnny Kuck of the USA has won the shot put with a throw of 52 feet ¾ inches. Second, also from the USA, is Herman Brix at 51 feet 8 inches, and taking home the bronze medal is Vilho Tuulos of Finland with a distance of 51 feet 6 ¼ inches. The gold medal in the hammer throw goes to Pat O'Callaghan of Ireland with a throw of 168 feet 7 inches. The silver medal was won by Ossian of Sweden at 168 feet 3 inches with Edmund Black of the USA taking the bronze medal. Now if you will look over to the discus ring. After two bad throws, Bud Houser, of the USA sent his third toss an unbelievable 155 feet 3 inches to win his third gold medal in only three attempts. Dr. Houser won gold medals in both the shot put and discus, the only events he entered, in the 1924 Olympics in Paris. The silver medal goes to Antero Kivi of Finland with a throw of 154 feet 11 inches, and young James Corson of the USA won the bronze medal with a distance of 154 feet 6 inches."

As James stuck out his hand to congratulate and thank Bud, his grin could not have been wider if he had won the gold medal."

Bud saw a small figure in a gray coat and hat sprinting across the field toward him. He braced for the impact as Dawn threw herself into his arms, and then he twirled her around and around until her feet were swinging almost straight out. "Aren't you the same snooty girl I saw at the track meet in Pasadena back in 1921?"

"You bet your life I am. Do you have any idea how badly you frightened me? I had to put my hands over my face during your last throw."

"If you missed it, I imagine it will be on the newsreel."

"Oh, I saw it. I peeked through my fingers."

"You even cheat when you're hiding your own face? How did you get in here?"

"The man at the gate told me I couldn't come through, but I was too fast for him."

"That's my little Trojan."

Chapter 53

Bud dropped the suitcases just inside the door, walked across the room, tumbled onto the couch, and pulled a pillow under his head. "Home at last. I'm never going on another long trip as long as I live."

"I thought you said you wanted to go back to Amsterdam some day."

"Oh yeah, I forgot. We'll take one more trip to Amsterdam, but that's all. Then we'll stay at home for the rest of our lives."

"You also said, 'Amsterdam is nice but I really would like to visit Paris again.' And, I heard you tell the swimmer, Yoshiyuka Tsuruta, that you would look him up when we go to Japan."

"Oh yeah, I forgot. We'll go to Amsterdam, Paris, and the Orient, and then no more traveling." He stretched his legs across the arm of the couch and groaned. "Will you please wake me up a week from Thursday?"

Dawn sprawled on their soft leather chair and asked, "What day is it now?"

"It's either yesterday or the day after tomorrow, I've lost track somewhere between the cruise across the Atlantic and the train ride to Los Angeles." His words were coming slower and his eyes were almost closed.

"Do you want to see who can sleep the longest?"

"That's a great idea, he slurred. "I think I can win that contest without much effort."

"You did it, sweetheart. You beat the best athletes in the world. I'm so proud of you. I really believe you could do anything you set out to do."

After a long pause, he said, "It's great to be married to a lady that believes in me."

"What are you going to do now that there are no more mountains to climb and dragons to slay?" When she received no answer, she asked. "Bud did you hear what I asked you?"

"Of course I heard you. There will always be mountains and dragons. They will just be less spectacular than winning the Olympics. In four years newspapers will be promoting a whole new group of athletes, and before we know it you and I will be forgotten."

She pulled herself up from the chair, stumbled a few feet to the couch and laid down with her back to him. Pulling his arm around her and snuggling up close, she asked, "Do you remember just before we boarded the ship in New York, when I was afraid of how much I was going to miss our old gang? Well, I won't deny that I missed Swede, and Glenn, and most of all Martha. She and I had so much fun in Paris. But, as great as Paris was four years ago, this trip was at least as good...I just loved Amsterdam, all the water and bridges and the friendly people...What a wonderful second honeymoon you provided for me...But, you know, now, I really am glad to be home...Our own little house...And, won't it be great sleeping in our own bed tonight...What would you think about going up to Lake Arrowhead for a few days rest before you go back to your office, honey? Honey...honey...Bud...Bud!"

Epilogue

In an era when athletes were not highly compensated for their talents, Dr. Houser's decision to forgo the offer from the owner of the Chicago Cubs baseball team and concentrate on graduating from the University of Southern California Dental School proved to be a wise choice. Following in Dawn's father's footsteps, he became dentist to many of the most prominent film stars of his day. He soon moved his office from 4106 West Pico Boulevard in Los Angeles to Vine Street in Hollywood.

Buddy Jr. was born to Bud and Dawn on September 1, 1932, and daughter, Bonnie, followed on October 22, 1935.

In addition to their home on Oak Drive in Hollywood, the Houser's owned a cabin on the lake in Lake Arrowhead, another vacation home in Palm Springs Canyon Country Club, and a home in Lake San Marcos. Over the years they remained avid USC fans. Wherever this attractive couple were, football season found them making the weekly trek to the Los Angeles Memorial Coliseum to join their old friends and cheer for the Trojans.

Bud and Dawn's children and grandchildren kept up the family tradition, receiving degrees from The University of Southern California.

When Dr. Houser wasn't giving celebrities more beautiful smiles, he and his family lived an active lifestyle. Bud loved to fish and hunt, and both he and Dawn became skilled golfers, with Bud carrying a four handicap. Dr. Houser became commodore of the Lake Arrowhead Yacht Club, where he participated in sail boat and power boat races. Both Bud and Dawn enjoyed water skiing and taught Buddy and Bonnie to ski while they were still small.

The Houser's remained friends with many of the athletes with whom he participated, attending sports and social events over many years.

From time to time, sportswriters from his era wrote articles in newspapers and magazines recalling the exploits of this striking man who had truly lived out the American dream.

Dawn died on March 3, 1987 at the age of 82. She was buried at Inglewood Cemetery. Bud lived to the age of 93. He was buried at Inglewood Cemetery alongside of Dawn.